MASTER YOUR LIFE WITH THE MASTERY SERIES

YOU CAN CHECK OUT the other books in the series , "Unleashing to Master the Power Within "below:

Scan below to learn about Ultimate Mindset Mastery Series

*Scan this QR code to
learn about Ultimate Mindset
Mastery Series*

*Scan this QR Code to learn
about Unleashing Mindset
Mastery Series*

Mindset Mastery Series

YOUR FREE GIFT

As a token of my thanks for taking out time to read my book , I would like to offer you a gift.
Download your Free PDF eBook
<u>10 Useful Ways of Talking To Any Body</u>
clicking the link
https://www.manjultewari.com/my-free-e-book/

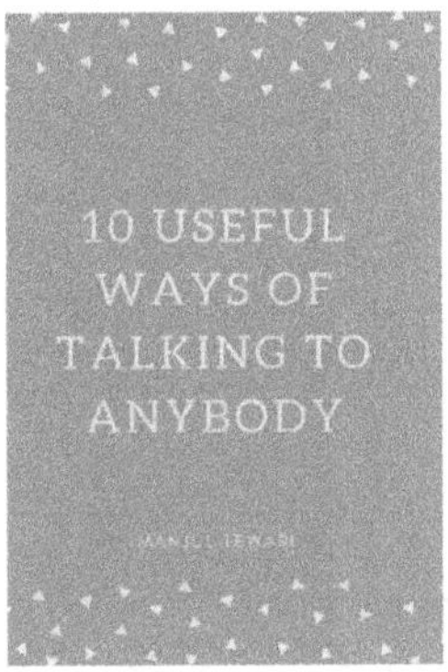

Ten Useful Ways of Talking To Anybody
OR

Scan this QR code to claim your free E Book.

*Scan this QR Code with your
smart phone and download your
free e book*

Published by Mr. Manjul Tewari
P-24, Engineer Park Apartment, Omega Sector-1
Greater Noida, UP, India 201308

Contents

CHAPTER ONE

INTRODUCTION

BENJAMIN WAS A GREAT person who once lived in the thriving city of Harmonyville. He was renowned for having an enviable intellect and an endless curiosity. When it came to thinking creatively and pushing the envelope of what was possible, Benjamin was incredibly gifted.

His experience served as a living example of the transformative potential of a creative mentality on both people and the environment. Benjamin had always been mesmerized by the busy sounds of the city, especially the metro's steady clatter.

One day, as he took the train to go home from work, he became aware of an oddity. The sound of the shaking rails and shrieking brakes seemed like music. Benjamin's thinking suddenly came up with an idea.

Motivated by his love of creativity, Benjamin set out to create a symphony out of the mundane train ride. With his bold concept to give subway commuters an original musical experience, he approached local officials.

His plan was mocked by many who thought it was just fiction. However, Benjamin didn't let that stop him since he had unflinching faith in his vision's ability to succeed. Ben set out to plan and carry out his creative endeavor using his own resources and a group of like-minded people. He worked tirelessly with musicians, engineers, and sound professionals to create a symphony of musical tones using the subway system. After several months, the day eventually came.

Benjamin presented Harmonyville with his masterpiece. A beautiful music that complemented the beat of the commuters' journey welcomed passengers as they boarded the trains. The once-boring drive had evolved into a remarkable musical experience. Benjamin's creative initiative quickly gained national recognition after word of it spread like wildfire.

People went to Harmonyville from all around the nation to hear the enchanted symphony for themselves. The city developed into a center of inspiration, drawing imaginative individuals and fostering an innovative culture. Beyond the symphony, Benjamin's business was a success.

Entrepreneurs and companies in Harmonyville started to embrace innovation as a result of his successes. Unprecedented levels of commercial success resulted from the flourishing of start-ups and the transformational shifts experienced by established businesses. The example of Benjamin served as a potent reminder of the influence that one individual's creative thought may have on an entire community.

In addition to changing the subway system, Benjamin also changed the course of countless other lives. His innovative thinking had sparked a creative upsurge and built an imaginative culture that had elevated Harmonyville to new heights.

As I set out on my own journey as an author and business owner, driven by an insatiable need for invention, I never forget this tale of Benjamin. I've seen firsthand the transformational power of creativity, from the busy streets of New Delhi to the digital worlds of self-publishing. As a self-published writer navigating the complexities of online platforms, I've been astounded by how innovation can expand the impact of words written with passion. This curiosity is exactly what inspired me to write "THE INNOVATIVE MINDSET."

I desired to not only perfect my own endeavors but also to assist others in stumbling through the turbulent currents of contemporary commerce. I hope that this book will help readers find their own unique routes to unrivaled achievement by igniting their creative spark. At its core, "THE INNOVATIVE MINDSET" is a compass, showing readers how to cultivate an inventive mindset and harness its dynamism to produce amazing business successes.

This book serves as a roadmap, encouraging people to transcend conventional limits, welcome change with open arms, and construct a future defined by daring ideas and resolute action. It does this via a tapestry of insights, tactics, and real-world experiences.

This book attempts to arm readers with the skills they need to not only survive but thrive in an ever-evolving business market, where innovation isn't a luxury—it's a prerequisite for unmatched success, by skillfully fusing the threads of creativity and entrepreneurship.

Readers of "THE INNOVATIVE MINDSET" will discover a wealth of advantages that promise to transform their outlook on work and life within its pages. They can expect the following transformative takeaways by fully absorbing the ideas and methods presented:

• Sharper Problem-Solving Skills: Develop a strategic and adaptive mentality to help you solve problems more efficiently by unlocking the ability to analyze problems from several perspectives. Recognize challenges as opportunities to develop original solutions.

• Increased Adaptability: Accept change as a constant and critical component of contemporary business. Learn strategies for making quick changes and thriving in the face of uncertainty so that you may gracefully navigate unfamiliar waters.

• Enhanced Creativity: Develop a wealth of creative thinking skills that will enable you to explore unknown mental realms and turn novel concepts into concrete realities.

• Integration of Innovation: Develop a thorough awareness of the part that innovation plays in promoting business expansion. Learn how to incorporate innovation into all aspects of your work, from product creation to customer interaction.

• Entrepreneurial Confidence: Establish a firm belief in your capacity to influence change and leave a lasting impression. Utilize your newly acquired self-assurance to take on risky endeavors that will take your organization to new heights.

• Effective Risk Management: Learn how to weigh prospective benefits against potential drawbacks in order to master the art of calculated risk-taking. To succeed through innovation, develop the ability to make well-informed decisions.

• Insightful Decision-Making: Develop your decision-making skills by drawing on a wealth of other viewpoints and concepts. Utilize your increased insight to create decisions that are in line with your creative vision.

• Improved Leadership: Develop your leadership skills by encouraging your team to venture into unexplored territory and by creating an environment that values creativity. Encourage others to accept change as a force for advancement.

• Sustainable Innovation: Create plans for fostering an inventive culture within your company so that creative thinking becomes a constant and essential part of your business operations.

• Trailblazing Success: In the end, readers can anticipate that turning an inventive attitude into observable business success will be the book's pinnacle accomplishment. Watch as your innovations transform your sector, spurring expansion and establishing new standards of excellence.

• Activities to Spark Your Creative Fire: Let's begin our trip with a series of stimulating exercises aimed at releasing your creative potential. Do you still play the "connect the dots" game from your youth? We're about to play it entirely differently. A banana, a compass, a typewriter, and a lighthouse are a few examples of seemingly unconnected words that you can draw across a page of paper using a pen. Create a tale that links these components together by drawing lines to connect them. Voila! You've just sparked cross-association, a crucial component of creative thinking.

• Follow these easy steps to learn the strategies that transform creativity into innovation: Innovation is the engine that moves us forward; creativity is the fuel.

Let's explore some useful tactics that fill the gap between undeveloped concepts and real-world results.

Meet Jane, a businesswoman who aimed to transform the travel sector. Armed with imagination, she envisioned a means to transform uninteresting layovers into rich cultural encounters. Her vision didn't, however, begin to take shape until she used a structured brainstorming process. Through' reverse brainstorming,' Jane and her group looked into methods to ruin her idea. Surprisingly, these "sabotage" ideas brought to light fresh perspectives and unexpected difficulties, leading her to a sophisticated, original solution.

• Everyday, learn Doable Tasks to Advance Your Journey

Let's face it: developing an inventive mentality takes time. Consistent work and deliberate techniques are essential for its success. I've dotted "Doable Tasks"—tiny tasks that nudge you toward new ways of thinking—throughout the book to help you. One of these tasks asks you to look at a problem from the viewpoint of a youngster and ask incessant "why" inquiries.

With this light-hearted approach, assumptions are peeled back to reveal the fundamental problems that demand for creative solutions. It is simpler to quickly summarize all the insights thanks to the key takeaways that are suggested at the end of each chapter.

In "The Innovative Mindset," we'll set out on a transformative trip that will test the way you think about issues, spark your imagination, and provide you the resources you need to promote innovation both within and across your company endeavors.

This book will explore both the artistic and scientific worlds, revealing the strategic frameworks that support successful invention while also examining the psychology of creativity. Fear not, though, as this is a dynamic journey where your active participation will be the wind in our sails. This is not a one-way discourse.

As readers take in the knowledge presented in " The Innovative Mindset," they will not only gain the skills necessary to prosper in the fast-paced business environment, but also go through a personal transformation that will enable them to approach problems with audacious creativity and to build a legacy of innovation-driven successes.

The phrase "innovate or perish" rings true in today's quick-changing and dynamic corporate environment.

Many examples from real-world businesses show how failing to innovate and adapt can have serious repercussions. Formerly a major player in the photography industry, Kodak clung to outdated film technology as digital photography advanced, ultimately contributing to their demise.

On the other side, Amazon's constant innovation has helped it to become one of the most valuable firms in the world, revolutionizing everything from e-commerce to cloud computing. This urgency is also shown by reliable studies. According to a Boston Consulting Group study, businesses that actively invest in innovation expand their revenues more quickly than their less innovative competitors.

Darwinism's tenets apply to the economic world as well: those who don't innovate will be displaced by rivals who do, as circumstances change and customer wants shift. With the speed at which industries are changing, it is crucial to be able to spot opportunities, try out novel concepts, and change course as necessary.

Blockbuster and Nokia's failures serve as a reminder that even industry heavyweights can stumble if they don't promote a culture of ongoing innovation. The option is clear in a day where disruption is the norm: either innovate to survive or face obsolescence and eventual extinction.

One truth shines out in an era where the average longevity of a Fortune 500 firm has fallen from 75 to just 15 years: innovation is essential to a company's ability to survive. According to Steve Jobs, former CEO of Apple, "Innovation distinguishes between a leader and a follower." The ability to build new paths, craft creative solutions, and give life to untested ideas is the currency of success in a world rife with change.

The desire to innovate is a requirement for everyone who dares to succeed in the face of constant change, whether they are a startup or an established industry powerhouse. The process of developing an inventive mentality is comparable to venturing into new territory, where the horizons of economic success are both alluring and intimidating and the landscapes of creation extend as far as the eye can see.

I want you to picture a world where your ideas dance on the border of possibility, where the ordinary is turned into the extraordinary, and where the seeds of invention you plant bear a harvest of unparalleled accomplishments as we set off on this journey together.

Welcome to "The Innovative Mindset: Unleashing Creativity, Fostering Innovation, and Achieving Unmatched Business Success." Therefore, keep in mind that you are holding more than just a book in your hands as we set sail on this adventure of innovation, creativity, and commercial success.

You possess a compass that will direct you through new territory, a toolbox that will enable you to modify your surroundings, and a wealth of knowledge that will inspire your quest toward unparalleled success.

Be ready to question conventions as we move through the pages that lie ahead, to accept ambiguity, and, most importantly, to unleash the hidden inventor within you. In the chapters that follow, we'll delve deeper into each aspect of the inventive mentality, breaking it down into its fundamental parts, and giving you practical advice and examples to help you move forward.

Keep in mind that innovation is a journey of growth and discovery, not a destination. So, let's set off on this amazing journey together, using curiosity as our compass and creativity as our sails. This journey promises to change the way you tackle obstacles as well as the narrative of your success.

The Innovative Mindset" inspires readers to accept their own original ideas, to challenge norms, and to pursue their passions without hesitation. Benjamin's tale served as a compelling reminder that having an inventive mentality not only paves the route for commercial success but also opens the door to a world of limitless opportunities.

9

CHAPTER TWO

HOW TO MAKE THE MOST OF YOUR PROBLEM-SOLVING SKILLS

"THE LOST MAP"

A BRAVE ADVENTURER BY the name of Maya once resided in the magical Himalayas. Maya had a reputation for being a daredevil who adored traveling to far-flung mountainous regions.

She set off on a voyage to a secluded valley that was reported to be surrounded by lush meadows and magical secrets and hold hypnotic and astounding beauty at the beginning of one summer.

Maya discovered the trail was poorly marked and the terrain was difficult as she made her way farther into the valley while clambering up and down the perilous path.

She had acquired a hand-drawn map from a local villager, but it was far from detailed, and she had depended largely on it when traveling through the thick jungles. There were only a few notable locations and a basic map of the valley. She was unable to pinpoint her precise position.

She encountered a catastrophe a few days into her voyage. Maya's overstuffed rucksack, which included among other things her priceless map, fell off her shoulders and slid into a roaring river as it descended a steep ravine.

The mountain river's fast surge swept away her link to the wonders of the valley as she gazed in agony.

However, Maya was not someone who gave up lightly. While most people would have turned around, defeated by the loss of their lone guidance. She made the choice to use her problem-solving abilities to seize this setback as a chance.

Maya paused to consider her predicament. From the pieces of the map she had already studied, she had a fundamental understanding of the topography of the valley. Additionally, she had a GPS unit and a compass in her little pack as part of her basic survival kit.

The final known location on the map was the first place she returned to. She then pointed herself in the appropriate direction using her compass. She was aware that there was a distinct mountain range in the valley, visible from most vantage points, to the north.

Maya took close attention to the natural landmarks surrounding her as she continued on her journey—a special rock formation, a certain kind of tree, and the position of the sun. These factors were her new compass as she adjusted to the shifting surroundings. These factors assisted in directing her in the proper route in this situation.

Maya communicated with the local communities she encountered while traveling. They imparted their understanding of the valley's topography, animals, and undiscovered water resources. Maya paid close attention and used this useful local knowledge to guide her course.

Maya was aware that she could make blunders along the way. She did not, however, let her fear of failing stop her. She retraced her steps and attempted alternate routes when she came across dead ends or impassable terrain.

Using her ability to solve issues and the information she had obtained; Maya continued her quest over the course of several weeks. She overcame difficulties, such as unforeseen weather changes and wildlife encounters, but she persisted.

Maya finally arrived in the secret valley she had set out to find on a foggy morning as the first rays of dawn peaked through the valley's lofty mountains. It was a stunning location unspoiled by contemporary society.

We can learn a lot from Maya's narrative on how to solve problems effectively.

Let's explore how problem-solving abilities may be used in numerous areas of life as we dig more into the lessons from Maya's journey.

1. **Flexibility and Adaptability**: Maya's success depended heavily on her capacity to adjust to shifting conditions. When addressing problems, this is being willing to modify your strategy when confronted with unforeseen difficulties. The world is dynamic, so being adaptable is essential whether you're tackling a challenging topic at work, navigating a personal relationship, or engaging in a creative activity like writing.

2. **Resourcefulness**: Maya used the tools at her disposal, including her compass, GPS, and the information she had obtained, to the fullest extent possible. We frequently have a variety of resources in our own life, both material and immaterial, that we might use to address issues. Information, equipment, skills, or even a strong social network could be among these resources. Utilizing these resources in original ways to come up with solutions is being resourceful.

3. **Local Expertise and Knowledge**: Maya enlisted the assistance of knowledgeable locals who lived in the region. It's beneficial to draw on the knowledge of professionals or individuals with appropriate experience while solving problems. Whether you're writing on a specific topic or encountering a barrier in your writing career, talking with experts or mentors can offer insightful advice and quick fixes for success.

4. **Trial and Error:** Maya overcame her fear of failing. She persevered despite setbacks, corrected her course after making mistakes, and learned from them. The road to success in problem-solving is frequently paved with setbacks and failures. Accepting a trial-and-error strategy enables us to grow, adapt, and ultimately discover workable answers.

5. **The need of persistence is maybe the most important lesson**: Maya's journey can teach us. At first it may appear as unsurmountable task but it is persistence and tenacity that go hand in hand that results in completion of our ultimate goal.

The Effect of Innovative Problem-Solving Beyond Business

Maya's journey serves as a microcosm for a more general truth: creative problem-solving skills are applicable in contexts well outside of the commercial sphere. They apply to all aspect of our life, from interpersonal interactions to volunteer work. We can overcome obstacles with resiliency and creativity if we embrace different points of view, adopt an innovative attitude, and put on our metaphorical thinking hats.

Let's remember that every obstacle presents an opportunity to improve your abilities, heighten your perceptions, and develop a robust mindset. You'll create novel solutions by fusing a symphony of viewpoints that have the potential to change not only your company but the entire planet.

Let's look at some credible research and sources that highlight the importance of problem-solving abilities in a variety of spheres of life, including school, the workplace, and personal growth.

Asking questions is an essential problem-solving ability, claim Alison Wood Brooks and Leslie K. John in a Harvard Business Review article. The article talks about study that shows that people who ask more questions, especially follow-up questions, are seen as smarter and more likely to be seen as leaders.

Similar findings were made by a long-term study that was published in Psychological Science, which tracked adolescents over a period of 30 years and discovered that the ability to solve problems in adolescence was a strong indicator of success in adulthood. Adolescents with strong problem-solving skills are more likely to graduate from college and have better employment chances.

Forbes also emphasizes the value of flexibility and problem-solving abilities in the contemporary workplace. The World Economic Forum report cited in the article identifies sophisticated problem-solving as one of the top skills needed in the workforce by 2025.

The idea of "small wins" in problem-solving is discussed in The New York Times. It is explained through research from Charles Duhigg's book "The Power of Habit" how breaking large difficulties into smaller, more manageable activities can improve problem-solving effectiveness.

The American Psychological Association sheds light on the significance of problem-solving skills instruction in the classroom. They highlight studies that demonstrate how structured problem-solving instruction can improve student and professional outcomes.

These reliable sources and research emphasize the link between successful problem-solving and enhanced career opportunities, perceived leadership, and general success.

Understanding Innovation: Unlocking the Heart of Change and Progress

To understand the importance of innovation let us recall the story of Suresh.

A visionary by the name of Suresh lived in the isolated village of Sundarpur, tucked away in the Indian state of Bihar. For a very long time, Sundarpur struggled with an electrical shortage that kept its citizens in the dark after sundown. The locals used expensive, hazardous kerosene lamps, which were also bad for the environment.

Suresh was resolved to rectify this after just moving back to his hometown after completing an engineering degree. He understood that Sundarpur required innovation to advance and become more enlightened.

Suresh noticed the region's year-round, plentiful sunlight one day while visiting his family's farm. It was a resource that was just waiting to be used. He was motivated and started learning about solar energy and its uses.

Suresh had many difficulties along the road. His ambitious initiative was met with skepticism by the villagers, and resources were scarce. Unfazed, he made a little investment by buying a few solar panels with his own money. Then he started placing them in important buildings throughout the area, such the community center, school, and medical facility.

A change started as soon as Sundarpur's new solar panels were exposed to the first sunlight. Now that there were electric lights in the school, kids could study after school. The clinic may store vaccines in the refrigerator and offer better medical attention. The community center held educational events and nighttime gatherings. The sun provided the energy for everything.

Suresh's concept caught the attention of NGOs and government organizations as word traveled quickly. They helped him develop the solar infrastructure such that it now serves every home in Sundarpur. The village was a shining example of sustainable development; it was no longer in the shadows.

This story captures the spirit of innovation:

1. **Finding Local Resources**: Suresh identified the untapped potential of local sunlight, demonstrating that innovation frequently begins with wise resource utilization.

2. **Overcoming Skepticism**: Innovators frequently encounter skepticism and resistance. Suresh's tenacity and early modest accomplishments convinced the skeptics.

3. **Beginning Small**: Innovation doesn't necessarily call for a lot of money. Suresh started out with a little project and added more solar panels over time.

4. **Impact on Community:** Genuine innovation has the capacity to change communities. Education, healthcare, and general quality of life all increased in Sundarpur as a result of its availability to clean, renewable energy.

5. **Collaboration**: When working on initiatives or soliciting funding from organizations or the community, innovators frequently work together with others.

The tale of Suresh demonstrates the immense influence of innovation, particularly when it comes to resolving urgent societal problems. It serves as a reminder that innovation isn't just about cutting-edge technology; it can also be as straightforward and effective as using solar energy to bring progress and light to a far-off community.

Human creativity is embodied in innovation, which is what propels development and change. It cuts through divisions, transforms industries, and ushers society into new eras of opportunity. Fundamentally, innovation is the skill of transforming abstract concepts into concrete realities that can fundamentally alter the way we live, work, and interact.

Examining the Innovation Spectrum

Innovation doesn't take the form of a single thing; rather, it exists in a variety of shapes, each with its own characteristics and ramifications. This spectrum, which spans small adjustments to game-changing innovations, illustrates the various ways that innovation drives development.

1. **Incremental Innovation:** Consistent Advancement via Refinement

Making incremental improvements to existing goods, procedures, or services is a continuous process. It's a methodical process that tweaks details without fundamentally changing the central idea. While initially appearing minor, these ongoing improvements add up over time to produce considerable gains.

Apple's iPhone evolution is an example of small-scale innovation. Each subsequent edition builds on the basis of the one before it, gradually providing improvements to the appearance, functionality, and use.

2. **Enhancing current offerings while maintaining innovation**

Optimizing current goods or services is the goal of sustaining innovation in order to keep them competitive. It entails enhancing qualities that appeal to customers while keeping up with changing preferences and technological advancements.

A sustained innovation is the automotive industry's move toward electric vehicles. In order to address growing environmental concerns, automakers are improving current car designs and converting them to electric powertrains.

3. **Innovative Disruption:** Rewriting the Rules

The term "disruptive innovation," made popular by Clayton Christensen, refers to innovations that transform markets and subvert conventional wisdom. It frequently begins by focusing on underserved markets or sectors and initially providing simpler, more approachable solutions.

By offering online streaming, Netflix upended the traditional video rental market, adapting to shifting consumer preferences and making brick-and-mortar rental shops obsolete.

4. **Innovative Breakthroughs:** Soaring into the Future

Paradigm-shifting discoveries that redefine whole industries are included under breakthrough innovation. These revolutionary advances introduce new ideas and technology, changing the environment and leading societies into uncharted waters.

The creation of the internet is a fundamentally innovative accomplishment. It radically changed the structure of contemporary civilization and transformed international communication, trade, and information transmission.

5. **Collaborative Innovation through Open Innovation**

Henry Chesbrough's concept of "open innovation" encourages external engagement to promote innovation. It recognizes that valuable concepts and know-how can come from outside of an organization's walls, fostering collaboration and co-creation.

The Connect + Develop program of Procter & Gamble is a prime example of open innovation. The business expands its innovation ecosystem by working with outside partners to gather ideas, technology, and expertise.

6. **Innovation in New Markets**: The Blue Ocean Strategy

Blue ocean innovation outperforms the competition by establishing new, undiscovered market niches. It entails presenting distinctive value propositions that appeal to non-traditional customers.

By fusing drama and acrobatics, Cirque du Soleil revolutionized the circus business and made traditional circuses obsolete while attracting a new audience.

7. **Innovative Discontinuity**: Radical Departures

Discontinuous innovation introduces products that defy accepted norms and disrupt core paradigms. It upends the current quo by bringing radical concepts that contradict accepted conventions.

Electric scooters have made a discontinuous innovation in urban mobility. These scooters present a novel way of transportation that modifies ideas about urban mobility.

8. **Frugal Innovation**: Impactful Simplicity

Frugal innovation concentrates on producing significant results with less resources. It was developed to address the need for solutions in contexts with limited resources, placing an emphasis on ease of use, accessibility, and cost.

A shining example of thrifty innovation is the Tata Nano, also referred to as the "people's automobile" in India. Through the streamlined design and production methods, it reimagined accessible personal transportation.

The dimensions of innovation have received a great deal of scholarly attention. Our understanding of market disruptions has been fundamentally altered by Harvard professor Clayton Christensen's pioneering work on disruptive innovation. His study demonstrated how established businesses frequently fail to adjust to disruptive changes, allowing newcomers to capture market share.

Christensen's book, "Innovator's Dilemma," described how firms might become victims of their own success by concentrating too much on maintaining innovation and ignoring disruptive opportunities. The study highlighted instances like Kodak's failure as a result of their resistance to adopt digital photography.

Similar to this, Eric von Hippel's study on "Lead User Innovation" emphasized the significance of including clients and users in the innovation process. His research showed that many innovations come from consumers who alter current products to suit their individual demands.

Research on "Reverse Innovation" by Vijay Govindarajan and Chris Trimble focused on the idea that inventions start in developing markets before expanding to developed countries. This phenomenon illustrates the possibility for innovation to come from unanticipated sources and questions the conventional flow of innovation.

Unleashing Brilliance Beyond Boundaries: The Innovative Mindset

The inventive mindset has repeatedly shown to be the thread that weaves brilliance beyond perceived boundaries in the dynamic tapestry of human success. As demonstrated by real-life examples of people and organizations that dared to break convention and embrace innovation, setting out on a path to cultivate this mentality opens doors to astounding possibilities.

• Airbnb: Rethinking Hospitality

Take a look at the history of Airbnb, which revolutionized how we see travel and lodging. In order to survive during the 2008 financial crisis, the company's founders converted their personal homes into guest rooms. They unintentionally pioneered a novel approach to hospitality as a result, upending the status quo of the hotel business. They transformed hardship into an opportunity by encouraging an inventive mindset, revolutionizing travel for millions of people around the world.

• Elon Musk's SpaceX: Revolutionizing Space Exploration

SpaceX is a prime example of how an inventive attitude can upend even the most established businesses. The Falcon 9 rocket, which is reusable and significantly lowers the cost of sending payloads into space, is the realization of Musk's dream of making space travel affordable. SpaceX reinvented space exploration and made it more practical than ever by rejecting traditional wisdom and embracing novel approaches.

• Tesla: Electrifying the Automotive Industry

Tesla, led by Elon Musk, contested the idea that electric vehicles were unattractive and unpractical. Tesla produced electric vehicles that sparked buyers' imaginations by putting an emphasis on performance, design, and innovation. This ground-breaking strategy not only upended the automotive industry, but also established new benchmarks for performance and sustainability, proving the value of pushing the envelope.

• Netflix: Redefining Entertainment

Netflix's revolutionary philosophy forever altered the entertainment industry. The business changed its business model from a DVD rental service to a streaming platform, thereby changing the way audiences consumed media. Netflix became a worldwide entertainment giant that posed a threat to conventional media models by using data analytics to tailor suggestions and creating original content.

• IBM's Watson: Pioneering AI in Healthcare

IBM's Watson is an excellent illustration of how the innovative attitude can permeate important industries like healthcare. By analyzing enormous volumes of medical data and delivering insights that help clinicians make more informed and timely decisions, Watson's cognitive computing capabilities changed medical diagnosis. Innovation can save lives, as demonstrated by the way technology and healthcare have combined.

These actual events highlight the significant benefits of cultivating an inventive attitude. They emphasize the idea that innovation is a concept that cuts across boundaries and isn't only restricted to one industry. Individuals and organizations can open up fresh opportunities for development and success by challenging presumptions, questioning norms, and accepting change.

The inventive attitude forces us to perceive obstacles as chances to learn and the uncharted as a blank slate for ground-breaking concepts. It's about realizing that the status quo is simply a starting point and that true brilliance comes from having the guts to travel untrodden territory. Remember that you come from a long line of dreamers who dared to dream big and changed the world as you set out on your own road of developing an inventive mentality.

Participate in the Adaptability Challenge

Let's take on a task to practice adaptability: pick a daily ritual—such as a commute to work, a morning routine, or an exercise schedule—and purposefully alter a crucial component. It can involve choosing a different route to work or switching from coffee to herbal tea. Observe how your mind responds. Do you feel anxious or uncomfortable? This exercise aims to train your brain to accept the unknown, a crucial component of the innovative mentality. It's not only about making small adjustments.

Learn to Push Yourself Beyond Your Comfort Zone

Our brains are programmed to look for familiarity and comfort. Although our ancestors benefited from having this attribute, it can impede creativity in today's constantly changing environment. Consider the first time you ate a food from a different culture. Although the strange flavors might have at first raised doubts, the courage to venture outside of your culinary comfort zone opened up new experiences and broadened your horizons. Similar to this, the inventive attitude thrives on forging ahead into the uncharted, accepting discomfort, and using it as a springboard for development.

How to Thrive in the Unknown by Mastering It

Think about the wonders of Pixar's animation. The company embraces risk-taking when producing each movie, venturing into uncharted technological and storytelling realms. They faced a significant obstacle during "Toy Story's production—an unfinished script with little time left to spare. The crew welcomed the chance to iterate and create instead of freaking out. They changed the story, creating new scenes and characters. The outcome? An animation revolutionized by a ground-breaking movie. This example demonstrates how even global industry leaders don't fear the unknown; rather, they thrive in it.

Developing Curiosity: Fuel for the Flame of Innovation

Have you ever watched a kid explore their surroundings? Their awe-filled eyes twinkle, and their never-ending barrage of "why" inquiries give the ordinary a vivid hue. This curiosity may wane as we get older and be replaced with the obligations of adult responsibilities. The inventive mindset, however, maintains that curiosity should never be restricted to childhood experiences.

Obtainable: The "5 Whys"

Ask "why" five times for each hurdle or issue you are currently dealing with, whether it be a business roadblock or a literary roadblock. With each "why," you'll uncover more information about the problem at hand by removing layers of presumption. By the fifth "why," you'll probably have reached the main issue. This method encourages you to investigate issues from multiple perspectives and come up with original solutions. It was inspired by children's inquisitiveness.

So, keep in mind that the inventive mentality is a fundamental tool that can be polished and sharpened as you delve further into the heart of innovation. It's a way of thinking that enables you to use curiosity as a lighthouse, adaptability as protection, and creativity as a weapon. It involves seeking out the excitement of the new, enthusiastically accepting difficulties, and combining the threads of tradition and change to create a tapestry of unheard-of achievement.

We'll discuss how to develop these elements, how to incorporate innovation into both your personal and professional life, and how to make the inventive mentality your most powerful ally in the chapters that follow. The road to release your greatness has just started, so buckle up, my friend.

The Revolutionary Effect of Innovation on the Current Business Environment

Innovation isn't just a buzzword in the fast-paced, dynamic corporate world of today; it's the key to success, expansion, and even survival. Companies that embrace innovation position themselves as industry leaders, able to reshape industries, fulfill changing client wants, and seize unexplored opportunities. As businesses use innovation to alter their processes, goods, and services, this revolutionary impact is visible across industries.

Industrial Revolutionaries: Forerunners of Change

The enormous impact of innovation on the current corporate landscape is vividly illustrated through a number of real-world situations. These businesses have upended established paradigms, forged new paths, and permanently altered their respective industries:

1. The retail sector was completely changed by Amazon's inventive abilities, which paved the road for e-commerce's supremacy. With its focus on the needs of the customer, frictionless online shopping, and ground-breaking ideas like one-click ordering, it has raised the bar. The launch of Amazon Prime, a cutting-edge membership service, raised consumer expectations and redefined customer loyalty.

2. Tesla: Electrifying the Automotive business:

Tesla's electric automobiles upset established standards in the automotive business, demonstrating how innovation can completely transform a sector. It transformed the driving experience through the incorporation of cutting-edge technology, environmentally friendly practices, and over-the-air updates. Beyond automobiles, Tesla's inventive attitude has an impact on battery technology and renewable energy options.

3. **Netflix: A New Era of Entertainment:**

By shifting from DVD rentals to online streaming, Netflix's novel business model upended the entertainment industry. By personalizing the content, its recommendation algorithms fostered a binge-watching culture. The company's unique content strategy completely altered the dynamics of traditional media by revolutionizing how shows and movies are made.

4. **Airbnb: Redefining Hospitality:**

By allowing people to rent out their spaces as hotels, Airbnb's platform completely changed the hospitality industry. This peer-to-peer strategy transformed the conventional hotel sector while introducing a unique way for travelers to experience countries. Community involvement and customized experiences were key components of Airbnb's creative business model.

5. **Apple:** The Design-Driven Innovator Apple transformed technology and consumer electronics with its unwavering dedication to design and user experience. The introduction of the iPhone, which combined computing, entertainment, and communication in one device, was a turning point. The advantages of seamless integration were clearly demonstrated by Apple's ecosystem of hardware, software, and services.

Innovative Mindset Benefits: Boosting Growth and Resilience

The benefits of developing an inventive mindset go far beyond immediate results. Companies that embrace innovation put themselves in a position for long-term success, resilience, and relevance in a business environment that is rapidly changing:

1. **Competitive advantage and market leadership**: By developing unique value propositions that appeal to customers, organizations can stand out in crowded markets through innovation. Apple has established

itself as the industry leader, retaining customer loyalty and exacting premium prices thanks to its constant innovation.

2. **Adaptation to Change**: Innovative businesses are better equipped to handle disruption. The switch by Netflix from DVD rentals to streaming is an excellent illustration of the significance of responding to shifting consumer tastes. These businesses foresee changes and adapt to suit new demands.

3. **Consumer-Centric Solutions**: Understanding and meeting consumer needs are given top priority in innovation. Amazon's dedication to improving customer experiences, cultivating loyalty, and recurring business is demonstrated through its use of data-driven insights to personalize recommendations.

4. **Employee Creativity and Engagement**: An innovative culture encourages employee creativity and engagement. Gmail and Google Maps are examples of inventions made possible by Google's well-known "20% time" policy, which permits employees to devote a portion of their workweek to personal projects.

5. **Industries can be disrupted by innovative companies,** which can make outdated business methods obsolete. Ride-sharing services like Uber were introduced, upending established taxi services and altering urban transportation around the world.

6. **Growth into New Markets**: Innovation opens the door to new markets and sources of income. Airbnb's platform demonstrated the possibility of lateral growth by going beyond rooms and providing one-of-a-kind experiences like local tours and workshops.

Academic analysis and research emphasize the practical benefits of innovation. The Global Innovation Index, released yearly by WIPO, INSEAD, and Cornell University, assesses nations' capacities for innovation and emphasizes how innovation drives competitiveness and economic progress.

Professor Clayton Christensen of Harvard Business School's research on "The Innovator's Dilemma" clarified the difficulties faced by established businesses when disruptive ideas appear. The study stressed the necessity for businesses to strike a balance between disruptive and sustaining technologies in order to remain resilient.

The Center for Information Systems Research (CISR) at MIT investigated why digitally progressive businesses outperformed their rivals. The study brought to light how business models, consumer experiences, and income streams are affected by digital innovation.

Inventiveness's Lasting Legacy

Innovation has an unmistakable revolutionary effect on the economic environment of today. Businesses that have an innovative attitude challenge conventional wisdom to produce new realities. The journey of innovation is characterized by tenacity, imagination, and the capacity to foresee possibilities that lay beyond the horizon, from trailblazing entrepreneurs to industrial giants.

The lessons from innovators like Amazon, Tesla, Netflix, Airbnb, and Apple resound as examples of the power of innovation as firms continue to develop. Businesses can not only prosper but also leave a lasting legacy of development and transformation by fostering an inventive culture, utilizing research discoveries, and remaining aware of shifting landscapes.

In conclusion, innovation drives a variety of transformative forms and serves as the lifeblood of progress. Each type of innovation—from subtle improvements to game-changing discoveries—contributes to the advancement of markets and society. Individuals and organizations can embrace change, affect the future, and create enduring effect by comprehending the subtleties of innovation's numerous facets and taking inspiration from well-established research.

Future Predictions: Embracing Adaptability

Remember that there are many different approaches to problem-solving as we draw to a close and look forward to the next stage of our trip. It's a dynamic process that changes with every obstacle, viewpoint, and creative answer. The symphony of thinking hats acts as an enduring tune that directs us to the core of original problem-solving.

The Landscape of Adaptability is the next stop.

We'll explore the adaptability landscape's ever-evolving terrain in the following chapter. We'll gain the skills necessary to thrive in the face of uncertainty as we learn how to sail new waters with grace and composure. Prepare to take your business initiatives to new heights by welcoming change as an ally.

In the following chapter, we'll explore the terrain of adaptability, where creativity serves as the compass and change is the only constant. We'll look at methods for savvily navigating new territory while embracing change as a fuel for development. Prepare to unleash the potential of adaptation and set out on a trip that will transform the way you view current business difficulties.

As we say goodbye to Maya's and Suresh's stories of triumph in problem-solving, we welcome the symphony of thoughts and viewpoints that will serve as inspiration for us as we continue to pursue unmatched commercial success via creativity and innovation.

Practical Training

Let's explore a number of useful activities that readers can include in their daily schedules to foster the innovative mindset:

1.Start your day by posing an intriguing question about something you see, such as a news headline, a work of art, or even the weather. get a list of three things that get you curious every day. It might be a query, an observation, or a subject you wish to investigate. This routine feeds your curiosity and motivates you to look for solutions and new perspectives throughout the day.

This straightforward routine sets the tone for a day full of curiosity and adventure. Keep a journal where you can record any creative thoughts that come to you during the day. There are no unworkable or crazy ideas. Regularly going over these entries can inspire more creativity.

2.Pick a random word—from a book, a dictionary, or an online word generator—and set a time limit for yourself to come up with as many associations, suggestions, or uses as you can. Brainstorm connections between any two items, concepts, or ideas that appear to be unconnected. Your capacity for association and creative thinking is improved by this practice. Cross-association and unexpected connections are encouraged by this practice, which is a crucial component of creative thinking.

3.Change Your Route: Take a purposefully different path on your daily walk or throughout your commute. This minor shift throws your routine off, makes you more adaptable, and makes you observe your environment differently.

4.Reverse Problem-Solving: Try to rephrase a typical difficulty you're facing as a question that starts with "How can I...?" For instance, if you're attempting to enhance productivity, ask, "How can I make the most of my time today?"

This encourages your brain to consider potential answers. Reverse brainstorming, often known as taking an issue you are experiencing and coming up with ways to make it worse, is another option. This unique strategy might help you identify potential hazards and point up creative solutions to those problems.

5.Open a dictionary or utilize an online random word generator for word ideas. Choose a word at random, then set the task for yourself to tie it to a challenge or project you're working on right now. Every day, set aside five minutes for unstructured drawing. As you put pen to paper, let your thoughts to wander. Drawing stimulates the formation of novel connections in the brain and can result in creative discoveries.

6. "No" to Assumptions: Make a list of all the presumptions you have about a subject you are familiar with. With the help of this activity, you can go further and consider the bases of your knowledge as you challenge each assumption with a "why."

7. Consider applying a successful concept or solution from a totally other industry to your current problem using analogous thinking. This activity promotes interdisciplinary thinking and inspires creative solutions. Find a parallel between a subject that interests you deeply and something completely unrelated every day. This exercise helps your brain form the strange connections that characterize creative thinking.

8.Put yourself in the position of a different person, such as a coworker, a client, or even a fictional character. Consider the issue or choice from their point of view. Your perspective will be widened by this practice, which also promotes empathy-driven solutions.

9.Consider extreme "what if" possibilities that are relevant to your project or aim. This exercise challenges you to go beyond the obvious, for instance, "What if we had no budget constraints?" or "What if our target audience was completely different?"

10. Daily Reflection: Think back on at least one occasion during the day when you handled a problem or circumstance with an inventive perspective. The solution? What failed? Your dedication to developing a creative mentality is strengthened by this reflection.

11.Take a quick break throughout the day to study your surroundings, whether it's a park, a café, or even your office. Make it a goal to pay attention to five new things that you haven't noticed previously. Your ability to identify possibilities and subtleties that others might overlook is sharpened by this activity.

12. The "Yes, And" Game: This activity fosters building upon ideas, resulting in more expanded and creative thinking, by replying to ideas or proposals with "Yes, and..." rather than "Yes, but..."

13. Unplug and observe: Designate a certain period of time each day to turn off all electronic gadgets. Use this time to take in your environment, watch people, or just think. This exercise cultivates mindfulness and heightens your sense of awareness of your surroundings.

14. Swapping Problems and remedies: Identify a problem you are having and make a list of possible remedies. After that, switch those solutions for a different problem you're tackling. Using an unorthodox strategy frequently results in surprising discoveries.

15. Learn three new talents each month that have nothing to do with your existing area of expertise or specialization. This might be something that piques your curiosity, like a skill, a language, a sport, etc. Your perspective will be widened, and this will encourage thinking across disciplines.

16. Daily "Why" Questions: Pick a subject or notion and ask "why" five times in a row, delving more deeply each time into the reasons for it. This method reveals hidden presumptions and may produce fresh perspectives or solutions.

These exercises are practical skills that you can use in your daily life, not just abstract ideas. Each activity is a stage in the process of teaching you how to think creatively. By continuously putting them into practice, you'll eventually cultivate the attitude that enables you to approach problems with inventiveness, adaptability, and a desire for novel viewpoints.

Keep in mind that consistency is the key to these exercises. You may gradually create an innovative mindset that lives on curiosity, adaptability, and creative problem-solving by incorporating them into your regular activities.

Main Points

Here, we go through the idea of the inventive mentality and how to cultivate it for amazing success in a variety of industries.

Introduction to the Innovative mentality: The innovative mentality may span the known and the unknown, tradition and transformation. It is a way of thinking that questions conventions, welcomes change, and aims to recognize possibilities in obstacles.

There have been many real-world instances of businesses and people that have adopted an innovative attitude to reshape their industries and succeed in extraordinary ways. Examples include how Airbnb revolutionized hospitality, how SpaceX transformed space exploration, how Tesla electrified the automotive industry, how Netflix revolutionized entertainment, and how IBM's Watson led the way in applying artificial intelligence to healthcare.

The innovative mindset is based on creativity and flexibility, which are its main components and methods. Novel ideas are produced by creativity, and ideas that are adaptable can change in a changing context. Similar to how a chef creates a special meal with a variety of ingredients, the inventive mentality entails fusing several viewpoints and concepts to produce something exceptional.

The inventive attitude promotes venturing beyond of your comfort zone and embracing the unfamiliar. Pixar's method of creating animated movies, which is marked by delving into unexplored territory, is an example of how even industry titans thrive on doing something novel.

Developing Curiosity: The innovative mindset is built on a foundation of curiosity. People can emulate children's inquisitiveness by asking "why" inquiries to investigate issues from various perspectives and generate original solutions.

Practical tasks: To foster an inventive mentality in daily life, several practical tasks have been provided. These activities include writing down random word connections, switching up routines, using similar thinking, and role-reversal practice, among others.

Here are some of them in more depth.

Start your day by asking an intriguing inquiry about something you observed, such as a news headline, a work of art, or even the weather. get a list of three things that get you curious. This routine encourages curiosity and discovery all day long.

Challenge yourself to come up with associations, concepts, or uses based on a word that was chosen at random. This activity improves associative reasoning and creative thinking.

Change Your Route: When performing daily tasks, choose a different path on purpose. This minor alteration upends the routine and promotes flexibility and new viewpoints.

Reverse problem-solving involves reframing difficulties as inquiries that start with "How can I...?" This strategy encourages inventive thinking about solutions and can result in novel concepts.

Connect a word that was chosen at random with a current undertaking or problem to generate fresh concepts. This method promotes cross-association and original ideas.

"No" to Assumptions: List the presumptions you have about a well-known subject, and then challenge each one with "why" to delve further and query basic assumptions.

Apply effective solutions from other disciplines to present problems using analogous thinking. This activity encourages inventive thinking and cross-disciplinary thinking.

To foster empathy-driven solutions and extend perspectives, consider problems from others' perspectives.

Pose extreme "what if" situations in relation to projects or goals to investigate options that go beyond the obvious.

Daily Reflection: Think back on times when you overcame obstacles by adopting a creative mindset. To strengthen your dedication to innovation, examine what worked and what didn't.

Play the observation game to improve your ability to identify opportunities and details by looking around and discovering five new things every day.

"Yes, And" Game: To expand on concepts and encourage creative thinking, answer questions with "Yes, and..." rather than "Yes, but..."

Disconnect from digital devices and pay attention to your surroundings to improve your mindfulness and awareness. Swapping problems and solutions might lead to unexpected discoveries. Try switching potential solutions between various problems.

Learn three new talents on a regular basis that have nothing to do with your existing field of competence in order to promote interdisciplinary thinking and broaden viewpoints.

Ask "why" five times each day to study issues from diverse perspectives and elucidate underlying presuppositions.

These useful drills are instruments that may be easily incorporated into regular routines. By regularly putting these into practice, people can cultivate an innovative mentality that is characterized by curiosity, adaptability, and creative problem-solving, improving their capacity to overcome obstacles and succeed in a variety of spheres of life.

With the help of these key insights, readers will be able to comprehend what the inventive mentality involves and how they can actively apply its principles to their daily lives. Readers are given the tools to foster their own unique attitude and realize their full creative potential by embracing curiosity, challenging presumptions, and exercising adaptation.

CHAPTER THREE

HOW TO DEVELOP AN INNOVATIVE MINDSET IN 10 EASY STEPS

EMBRACING CHANGE: THE ENTREPRENEUR'S DILEMMA

A CHARMING BOOKSTORE CALLED "The Pages' Haven" stood as a tribute to the power of adaptability in the center of a bustling city. The Pages' Haven held its ground amidst the imposing structures and busy streets, having deftly ridden the wave of change. It served as a source of motivation for business owners who were struggling to accept change in an environment where businesses are always changing.

The Innovative Mindset: An Exploration

Meet Rahul, a budding businessman who loves reading and who inherited The Pages' Haven from his parents. He had a choice to make when he took over the bookstore: change or vanish. The traditional bookshop business model had been threatened by the emergence of digital books and internet merchants. Innovation was clearly the key to The Pages' Haven's survival and would define its future.

It took more than just integrating new technology for Rahul to create The Pages' Haven into a thriving literary cluster; it also required developing a creative attitude that could withstand challenges and seize chances.

Step 1: Adopt Curiosity and Exploration

Accepting curiosity as a motivating factor is the first step in developing an inventive mentality. Entrepreneurs must constantly ask "why" in order to find new things, much like children do. The simple question "Why does a bookshop have to be limited to selling books?" set Rahul on the path to discovering other opportunities, such as presenting author talks and introducing items with literary themes.

Step 2: Encourage a Climate of Unafraid Experimentation

A culture that values experimenting fosters innovation. Rahul understood that failing wasn't a setback but rather a way to advance. He transformed The Pages' Haven into an innovation lab by encouraging a culture where his staff felt free to innovate. They attempted novel book displays, held pop-up gatherings, and even tested a virtual loyalty scheme.

Step 3: Accept Failure as a Learning Catalyst

Failures turned into lessons that fueled Rahul's travels. The third phase entails accepting failure as a necessary step toward success rather than as a sign of defeat. Rahul learned about client preferences from each unsuccessful book display, just as each experiment yielded insightful results. The basis of his innovative thinking was his capacity to iterate and learn from mistakes.

Step 4: Develop cross-disciplinary thinking

Innovation frequently occurs where various fields converge. The fourth step urges business owners to look outside of their industry. Rahul merged the visual and literary arts by working with regional artists to produce book-inspired artwork. This interdisciplinary approach gave The Pages' Haven fresh life and drew in a wide range of customers.

Step 5: Seek out Opportunities in Change

The pulse of innovation is change. Entrepreneurs need to welcome change, not as a threat but as a chance to advance. Rahul noticed how e-books were altering reading patterns and came to the conclusion that embracing technology may improve the experience of visiting a bookstore. He installed e-book vending machines, converting The Pages' Haven into a venue where the physical and digital worlds coexisted.

Step 6: Developing a Growth Mindset

Innovation grows best in an environment where people have a growth mindset. The sixth step entails accepting obstacles as opportunities for development. Rahul and his group addressed difficulties with optimism, seeing them as passing humps. This kind of thinking encouraged them to consider nontraditional alliances and start joint events with adjacent cafes and theaters.

Step 7: Promote Team-Based Innovation

Diverse minds coming together can boost innovation. The seventh step emphasizes fostering group innovation. "Literary Hackathons," which Rahul founded, brought together authors, techies, and designers to produce cutting-edge literary experiences. This strategy not only produced original thoughts, but it also helped to build a sense of community around The Pages' Haven.

Step 8: Change to Suit Customers' Needs

Innovation is a conversation with consumers. The eighth step underlines how critical it is to pay attention to consumer needs and make appropriate adjustments. Rahul talked with clients about their reading tastes, which helped him choose books and schedule events. This focus on the needs of the client made sure that The Pages' Haven stayed current and connected with its readers.

Step 9: Adore inclusion and diversity

Through the introduction of new viewpoints, diversity fosters innovation. The ninth step is embracing diversity in both ideas and demographics. Rahul ran thematic book clubs that read works from many cultures and viewpoints. This appreciation of diversity widened the bookstore's appeal and enhanced its selection.

Step 10: Honor Small Successes and Milestones

Innovation is a process, not a final product. Step ten places a strong emphasis on appreciating both little successes and large achievements. Rahul recognized and praised each successful innovative attempt, from the beginning of a community reading festival to the achievement of a new book display. These festivities gave the team fresh life and spurred their desire to keep innovating.

Finding Your Way Through the Sea of Change: Increased Adaptability

Heightened flexibility played a significant role in Rahul's journey toward developing an inventive mentality. The Pages' Haven evolved from a conventional bookstore into a vibrant literary center that held art exhibitions, literary festivals, and participatory storytelling events.

We will investigate methods for enduring uncertainty as we navigate the sea of change. The way forward will become clearer with examples from the real world of businesses that successfully changed course during crises. We'll go into the practice of adaptable thinking so you have the skills necessary to see the bright side of change.

As we set off on a trip that will equip you to thrive in the face of uncertainty, get ready to embrace the power of adaptability, just as Rahul changed The Pages' Haven from a standard bookshop into a thriving literary haven of creativity. Let's look at one more example of adaptability.

"The Lesson of the Bamboo"

A wise old man named Asha lived in a peaceful community tucked away deep amid the jungles of northeastern India. She was well-known around the area for her fortitude in the face of adversity, and her life was a tribute to adaptability.

The community experienced an unexpected drought one summer. The once-prolific river that provided water for their crops had diminished to a trickle. The peasants were fearful because their way of life was in jeopardy. They flocked around Asha in search of direction.

With her trademark composure, Asha asked the locals to accompany her into the surrounding bamboo grove. She started out by imparting a wise lesson as they made their way through the tall bamboo stalks.

Asha directed attention to the long, slender plants that were softly swaying in the breeze, saying, "Observe the bamboo." "The bamboo is the one that teaches us the art of flexibility in times of uncertainty."

The inflexible trees snap under the force of the storm, she explained, but the flexible bamboo bends and endures. Asha continued, "Adaptability, my dear friends, is not about fighting change. The key is to embrace flexibility and find strength in it.

The peasants became adaptable as a result of her comments. They changed the way they farmed, dug deeper wells, and pooled their resources. They eventually prospered as well as survived the drought. Their improved adaptation served as a source of resiliency for succeeding generations.

This story powerfully illustrates the value of flexibility in the face of uncertainty:

1. **Embracing Change:** Embracing change rather than fighting it is a crucial component of adaptability, much as the bamboo bends with the wind.

2. **Learning from Nature:** Nature frequently teaches us important lessons. Here, the bamboo instructs us to be adaptable and resilient in the face of adversity.

3. **Resilience through Adaptability**: The villagers prospered as a result of their ability to adjust to their changing environment, demonstrating how adaptability may result in resilience and even development during difficult times.

4. **Community and Collaboration**: The villagers cooperated, sharing resources and expertise, which is frequently a key component of adaptability.

5. **Transferring knowledge:** Asha's knowledge made sure that the community was better prepared for future uncertainty by passing down the importance of adaptability to future generations.

This narrative serves as a reminder that adaptability and flexibility are vital skills to have while embarking on unknown adventures, whether they involve writing and self-publishing or any other effort. By accepting change and changing course as required, we can flourish in the face of life's storms like the bamboo. In this sense, flexibility develops into a potent tool for flourishing in the face of uncertainty rather than merely surviving.

But let's skip the filler and tired platitudes. The inventive mindset involves establishing a mindset that actively seeks possibilities in challenges, refuses to be constrained by tradition, and feeds on the pleasure of converting the unusual into the exceptional. It doesn't involve donning outlandish headgear or coming up with crazy plans. It's a skill that everyone can cultivate and improve, just like learning a recipe or a musical instrument. It's not only a quality of the select few.

Discover the Ingredients and Methods in the Recipe for Innovation.

The inventive mindset can be split down into its essential components and methods, much like a cook follows a recipe. Creativity and adaptability are two essential components of innovation at its foundation. Novel ideas are generated by creativity, and adaptation ensures that these ideas can develop and flourish in a changing environment. Imagine flexibility as the wind that propels a firework to new heights and creativity as the spark that ignites it.

Understanding the Cost of Resistance to Change: Lessons from the Abyss

In the background of innovation's success stories, there are cautionary tales of organizations that fought change and ultimately failed. There are individuals who choose to adhere to obsolete models, which will lead to their downfall, just as The Pages' Haven welcomed change to grow.

The Blockbuster example is one of these cautionary tales. Blockbuster was once a well-known name in movie rentals, but its resistance to change to digital streaming was catastrophic. Blockbuster maintained its brick-and-mortar renting strategy while streaming platforms gained popularity, failing to anticipate the fundamental change in consumer behavior. The business ultimately failed because it refused to shift course and adopt digital distribution, reflecting the price of reluctance to adapt in a quickly changing environment.

Companies that mastered adaptation overcame adversity

There are success stories that have overcome adversity among the tales of decline. These businesses accepted change and adjusted their strategy to fit the new environments.

Take Netflix, which first offered DVD rentals. Netflix changed its business strategy and adopted digital distribution after seeing the potential of streaming. With this change, it went from being a DVD rental service to a major global streaming player, completely changing the entertainment landscape. Netflix advanced to the forefront of innovation thanks to its capacity to embrace change and predict consumer preferences.

Missed Call by Nokia: A Story of Lost Innovation

Blockbuster shared a similar demise with Nokia, a brand previously closely associated with mobile phones. Nokia's aversion to change was obvious as smartphones entered the market. Although the corporation was a leader in mobile technology, it was slow to embrace the smartphone revolution. Its unwillingness to modify its operating system and user interface caused its market share to rapidly fall. The tale of Nokia serves as a warning that even powerful figures in an industry can lose favor if they don't change with the times.

Apple's Fortitude: Trailblazing Innovation

Apple is a prime example of the strength of adapting, in sharp contrast to Nokia's fate. In 1997, Steve Jobs came back to Apple, which was on the verge of going out of business. Jobs guided Apple through a transformational process as opposed to fighting change. He reworked the company's product portfolio, unveiled cutting-edge creations including the iPod, iPhone, and iPad, and introduced creative designs. Apple's propensity for anticipating market trends and changing its product line-up has cemented its position as a technical titan.

The Retail Evolution: Mastering Change with Amazon

The emergence of e-commerce resulted in a fundamental change in the retail sector. While many conventional stores found it difficult to change, Amazon grasped the chance to revolutionize the way people shop. Amazon's dedication to innovation resulted in the launch of Amazon Prime, which revolutionized the online shopping experience by offering quick shipping and streaming services. The business transformed from an online bookstore to a worldwide marketplace thanks to its adaptable change management strategy, changing how customers interact with goods and services.

Adaptation Lessons: Managing Uncertainty

The tales of Blockbuster's demise and Apple's success, Nokia's plight and Amazon's rise, and others, provide priceless insights. They emphasize the value of embracing change, spotting trends, and making adjustments as needed. Companies who embraced an inventive mentality and realized that change is an opportunity for growth rather than a danger prospered.

Keep in mind that as we explore the idea of enhanced flexibility, everyone has the capacity to change course and prosper under pressure. You may guide your company toward resilience and success by learning the skill of adaptive thinking and picturing successful outcomes even when change is present.

Findings from Research on Adaptive Thinking

Research studies provide insightful information about how adaptable thinking affects people and businesses. Let's examine some empirical facts that demonstrate the importance of embracing change and creative approaches.

Success of IBM's Reinvention: IBM's path is a great illustration of a business that adopted adaptive thinking. The business saw diminishing profitability and market share in the 1990s. To establish itself as a solutions provider, IBM, however, changed its emphasis from hardware to services and software. According to a Harvard Business Review research, IBM was able to restructure its business model thanks to this strategic pivot, which enhanced profitability and sustained success.

The Effects of Growth Mindset People with a growth mindset are more likely to use adaptive thinking, according to psychological studies. According to a research in the "Journal of Applied Psychology," people who thought they could improve their skills via hard work and education were more adaptable to change and innovation. This way of thinking enhanced performance in all areas, including problem solving.

Netflix's Data-Driven Innovation: The success of Netflix is directly related to its data-driven method of adaptive thinking. According to a McKinsey & Company research, Netflix's capacity to gather and analyze user data allowed them to generate original programming that appealed to a variety of audiences and to customize content recommendations. This data-driven innovation was crucial in helping Netflix grow into a major streaming powerhouse.

Warning Tales of Change Resistance

On the other hand, there have been occasions where people and businesses suffered greatly as a result of opposition to change. These cautionary tales highlight the significance of adaptable thinking in light of changing environments.

Kodak's Missed Opportunity: Kodak, a once-famous name in the photographic sector, serves as a warning about the dangers of not adapting. An analysis of Kodak's demise in the "Journal of Strategic Marketing" noted its reluctance to adopt digital photography as a crucial issue. Despite developing the first digital camera in the 1970s, the company took its time switching from film to digital, which ultimately contributed to its demise.

Leadership's Crucial Role in Adaptive Thinking: Leadership is essential for fostering adaptive thinking inside businesses. The "Journal of Change Management" published a study that looked at how leadership style affects an organization's capacity for change. According to the study, leaders that supported a climate of experimentation, welcomed change, and encouraged taking risks were more likely to inspire adaptive thinking within their employees.

The Personal Cost of Resistance: Individually, opposing adaptive thinking can impede success in both job development and personal improvement. According to a research by Stanford University's Center for Research on Education Outcomes, pupils who had a fixed mindset—a conviction that their abilities are unchanging—were less likely to rise to the occasion and adopt novel learning techniques. Due to this entrenched perspective, they were unable to realize their full academic potential and unable to adapt to changing environments.

Lessons from Adaptive Leaders

There are many instances of people and organizations who have effectively adopted adaptive thinking. Their stories provide priceless insights into the value of adaptability and creativity.

A case study on Steve Jobs and Apple's evolution from a struggling business to a leading innovator examined how Apple changed under Steve Jobs' leadership. According to the report, Steve Jobs' willingness to change the company's emphasis, launch new product lines, and embrace design innovation was crucial in reviving Apple's brand and profitability. So is Jeff Bezos' leadership style, which places an emphasis on long-term goals over short-term advantages.

The Psychology of Adaptive CEOs: A study by the University of Chicago Booth School of Business looked at the psychological characteristics of CEOs who led their organizations through difficult periods. The study discovered that CEOs who were adaptable displayed high levels of cognitive flexibility and were receptive to novel experiences. These qualities allowed them to develop creative solutions and make timely strategic moves.

As you examine these research findings, keep in mind that adaptable thinking is a practical ability that can promote both individual and group achievement. You may arm yourself with the skills necessary to succeed in a business environment that is constantly changing by studying the experiences of organizations and people who have embraced change.

Key Learnings:

- Embrace Curiosity: Having an open mind and being willing to challenge the current quo are the first steps in creativity. New opportunities and ideas might result from curiosity.

- Create a culture of fearless experimentation by encouraging people to try new things and treating setbacks as a chance to improve.

- Learn from Failure: Failure is not a setback; rather, it is a stride toward success. Accept it, consider it, and use it to improve your strategy.

- Cross-Disciplinary Thinking: Innovations frequently appear where various disciplines converge. Work with others who have different perspectives to inspire innovation.

- Embrace change as an opportunity rather than as a threat if you want to advance and get better. In a dynamic environment, embracing change can help you remain relevant.

- Having a growth mindset means approaching problems with optimism and seeing failures as transient obstacles to progress.

- Encourage the coming together of different ideas to create a collaborative environment that stimulates invention.

- Customer-Centric Approach: Pay attention to your consumers' wants and preferences and modify your offers accordingly.

- Diversity & Inclusion: Be open to a range of ideas and demographics, as this can produce new insights and richer services.

- Celebrate minor Wins: To increase morale and motivation, acknowledge and recognize every accomplishment, no matter how minor.

- Creativity and Adaptability: Innovation is a byproduct of both of these traits. While adaptability makes them survive in a changing world, creativity generates new ideas.

- Lessons from Cautionary Tales: Take a cue from organizations that fought change and suffered decline, like Blockbuster and Kodak. Recognize the expense of not adjusting.

- Triumph over Adversity: Businesses like Netflix, Apple, and Amazon were successful because they accepted change and modified their business plans to suit shifting market conditions.

- Role of leadership: Strong leadership is essential for encouraging adaptable thinking within businesses.

- The Strength of Flexibility: Adaptive thinking is a practical talent that can promote both individual and group achievement. Learn from people and businesses that accepted change and prospered.

- These conclusions emphasize the value of a customer-centric perspective, experimentation, adaptability, and curiosity in developing a creative mindset. They also stress how important it is to learn from both failures and successes in the corporate sector.

Workouts to Improve Your Adaptive Thinking

Exercise 1: The Alternate Scenario

Ask yourself what would happen if your industry or business land-scape drastically changed in this alternate scenario. Consider a future in which there are no more physical storefronts if you work in the retail industry, for instance. How might you adjust? Create a list of tactics and creative fixes that would help your company not just survive but also flourish in this fictitious world.

Exercise 2 : "The Trend Forecaster's Hat."

Put on your "trend forecaster's hat" and investigate new trends in your industry. Find changes in market dynamics, technical improvements, and customer behavior. Think about the potential effects these trends could have on your company in the future. Think of creative methods to proactively modify your tactics, goods, and services to reflect these anticipated changes.

Exercise 3: The Pivot Simulation:

Choose a case study from the past of a business that successfully changed course during a crisis. Examine the elements that contributed to their adaptation's success. Imagine that you are in a situation similar to this, where unexpected events are causing your industry to change. Utilize the case study's lessons to create your own strategic pivot plan.

Exercise 4: The Cross-Industry Inspiration

Look for inspiration outside of your own field. Analyze how a successful company that operates in a totally different industry has adapted to the times. Think about how you could apply these tactics and techniques to your own company. This activity inspires you to use your imagination and find novel approaches to your problems.

Exercise 5: The Future situation

Create a storyboard or other visual representation of a future situation in your sector. Draw attention to potential problems, obstacles, and possibilities. To convey this futuristic landscape, use pictures, keywords, and descriptions. Next, list the essential qualities and abilities you would need to succeed in this situation. This activity gives you the tools you need to adjust while also assisting you in visualizing various future courses.

Exercise 6: "Reverse Brainstorming"

Gather a group of coworkers or friends and perform a "reverse brainstorming" session. Focus on coming up with methods to exacerbate an issue rather than coming up with solutions. This paradoxical strategy frequently results in the discovery of potential traps and difficulties. Identifying these difficulties can help you come up with creative solutions and successful adaptation strategies.

Exercise 7: The Positive Outcome Visualization

Consider a recent or present difficulty that your company is facing. Consider how you want that struggle to go now. Imagine how the difficulty becomes a chance for development, innovation, and achievement. This practice encourages adaptive thinking by teaching your mind to look for solutions in the face of difficulty.

Exercise 8: The Collaborative Adaptation Workshop

Organize a workshop with coworkers or other entrepreneurs . Describe a widespread issue that your sector is now facing. Encourage the participants to contribute their insights, stories, and solutions. This collaborative method exposes you to other points of view and encourages inventive ideas to effectively adapt.

Exercise 9: The "What If" Scenario Generator

Use the power of "what if" questions to explore different possibilities. Write down your responses and potential solutions to hypothetical concerns like, "What if our principal distribution channel became obsolete?" or "What if client tastes suddenly changed." You can respond to unforeseen changes with confidence after completing this practice.

Exercise 10: "Innovation Journal"

Keep a "Innovation Journal" in which you record your industry-related observations, trends, and discoveries. Update it frequently with articles, case studies, and concepts that catch your attention. As you come up with adaptive strategy ideas, get inspiration from your notebook. Your mind will remain open to change and innovation thanks to this constant practice.

As you begin these exercises, keep in mind that you can develop your adaptive thinking skills over time. By continuously putting these techniques into practice, you'll become more adept at navigating uncertainty with agility, accepting change as an opportunity, and imagining a time when your company flourishes in the face of changing environments.

A study on Jeff Bezos and Amazon's agility that appeared in the "Strategic Management Journal" examined how well Amazon was able to adjust to shifting market conditions. According to the report, Amazon's agility is a result of its capacity to experiment, embrace iterative processes, and quickly change course in response to user input. One factor that contributed to Amazon's adaptive success.

CHAPTER FOUR

WHY IS IT IMPORTANT TO FOSTER YOUR OWN CREATIVITY

EXPLORING CREATIVE SOURCES

A VENTURE INTO THE Unknown:

Arjun lived in the throbbing metropolis of New Delhi, tucked away in the din of daily existence. Arjun was a self-employed novelist with a strong urge to tap into the depths of his creative well and venture into undiscovered realms of fantasy. His quest involved self-discovery, ingenuity, and an unrelenting search for artistic perfection.

Arjun's narrative began with the awareness that he wanted his writing to go beyond the commonplace and have a profound impact on people all around the world. He did, however, come up against a well-known foe: writer's block. His creative thoughts looked distant, and his imagination seemed like a dry desert. Arjun set out on a trip to access his untapped inspiration reserves in an effort to escape this creative rut.

The Curiosity Catalyst

The desire to discover the secrets of his mind's imaginative crevices was what initially motivated Arjun on his adventure. He started by immersing himself in a wide range of activities, such as seeing art galleries and taking in the scenery. Each interaction served as a spark, awakening his interest and luring his imagination into uncharted territories.

Arjun understood that fresh experiences and viewpoints are essential to creativity. He began keeping an observational notebook in which he noted the subtleties of his environment, the talks he had with strangers, and the feelings sparked by various stimuli. He learned to draw inspiration from the commonplace and elevate it to the spectacular by practicing thoughtful observation.

The Cross-Association Canvas

As Arjun continued on his adventure, he came across the idea of cross-association, a strategy employed by creatives to make links between ideas that at first glance appear unconnected. This gave him the idea for a novel exercise in which he would choose two unrelated things or ideas at random and set himself the task of weaving them together into a narrative.

He pulled "a bicycle" and "a lighthouse" one day from his creative well. A tale of a lone traveler traversing untamed terrain, led by the far-off beacon of a lighthouse, evolved as he thought about their link. This activity not only inspired his creativity, but it also showed how cross-association may help people bridge the gap between the known and the unknown.

The Power of Uncharted Territory: Embracing Uncomfortable Situations

The trip of Arjun wasn't without difficulties. He came to the realization that real creative development needed him to leave his comfort zone and venture into unfamiliar waters. He immersed himself in genres he had never before investigated, such as historical romance and science fiction. He had to face his own prejudices and presumptions as a result of this exploration, which broadened his perspective.

He came across a news report about a vanished civilization one day. He set out on a quest of investigation and fantasy because of the mysteries it held. He included this historical context into his story in order to give it authenticity and depth. He learned from this experience that expanding one's horizons opened the door to limitless creativity.

The Creative Spirit's Tenacity

Arjun's path served as a monument to the creative spirit's tenacity. He had changed from a self-conscious writer to a writer who bravely faced the unknown. He had used his creative well to produce concepts that cut across time periods and nations. His works struck a chord with readers everywhere, taking them to other places.

Cross-association was Arjun's distinctive strategy for incorporating unexpected themes into his stories and entrancing readers with the power of their untapped imagination. He had discovered that creativity was a fire that sprang out of curiosity, discomfort, and the fortitude to explore uncharted territory.

A Tradition of Innovation

The voyage of Arjun has completed a round. His tales were no longer confined to the pages of his books; they were now a living example of the effectiveness of using one's imagination to go to undiscovered regions.

His readers were in awe at the complexity of his characters, the richness of his stories, and the relevance of his topics.

Beyond his own writing, Arjun left behind a legacy that encouraged other aspiring authors to embrace their creative potential and go out on exploratory trips. His method of cross-association had established itself as a mainstay in writing classes, kindling the imaginations of numerous students.

Arjun came to the conclusion as he reflected on his trip that creativity was not a limited resource but rather an inexhaustible supply waiting to be discovered. He explored uncharted territory with each narrative he wrote, catching the essence of the mysterious and turning it into a blank canvas for creativity. His adventure served as a reminder that the human spirit was capable of going beyond limitations and that those with the courage to venture into the undiscovered realms of imagination would find limitless opportunities.

How to unleash our creative potential

Innovation is at its core a creative process. Let's now investigate methods for releasing our creative reserves and venturing into uncharted imaginal realms. Each person possesses creativity, the source of invention and growth, waiting to be developed and utilized. It acts as the catalyst for ground-breaking ideas, drives personal development, and reshapes the world. Developing your creative potential and cultivating an exploratory and inventive attitude require a variety of techniques and viewpoints, which you might embrace.

1. Develop Curiosity and an Open Mind:

The doorway to creativity is curiosity. Accept a never-ending curiosity in the world and a desire to comprehend the subtleties and complexity of many topics. Explore subjects outside of your comfort zone to make connections between concepts that at first glance seem unrelated.

Curiosity about the natural world drove renowned scientist Richard Feynman to make revolutionary discoveries about quantum physics.

2. Accept Different Points of View:

Surround yourself with a variety of viewpoints and ideas. Engage with people from various disciplines, industries, and backgrounds. Because of his exposure to a variety of artistic inspirations while in college, Steve Jobs was able to incorporate calligraphy into Apple's design philosophy, enhancing the aesthetic appeal of Apple products.

3. Make Your Environment Inspirational:

Your environment is crucial in fostering creativity. Create a mental and physical environment that inspires your creativity. Leonardo da Vinci, a Renaissance polymath, had a workshop full of books, scientific equipment, and works of art that fed his diverse creativity.

4. Reflection and mindfulness exercises:

Practices of mindfulness improve awareness, concentration, and self-reflection— are essential components of fostering creativity. You can access your inner self through meditation and mindfulness and discover original insights. We may thank Steve Jobs' mindfulness exercises for the zen-like simplicity of Apple's product designs.

5. Accept Failure as a Learning Experience:

Failure is a stepping stone for creativity, not a barrier. Accept setbacks as chances to improve, iterate, and learn from them. Thomas Edison made thousands of unsuccessful attempts in his quest to create the light bulb, each of which helped him achieve success in the end.

6. Creatively Use Constraints:

By requiring you to come up with creative solutions, constraints encourage innovation. Accept constraints as challenges that inspire your imagination. Early computers had limited processing capability, which spurred developers like Bill Gates to create creative software solutions.

7. Divergent thinking exercises:

Divergent thinking promotes investigating several options and points of view. Without passing judgment, practice brainstorming and idea generation. The innovation culture at 3M encourages staff members to spend 15% of their time working on original initiatives. As a result of this policy, a worker's experimenting with adhesive technology gave rise to the iconic Post-it Notes. This approach gave rise to the "Post-it Note."

8. Investigate interdisciplinary learning:

To give your thoughts new views, learn from many disciplines. Cross-disciplinary understandings can result in creative discoveries. Early Apple computers featured exquisite font thanks to Steve Jobs' interest with calligraphy.

9. "Four C Model of Creativity"

In order to develop creativity, Paul Torrance and Mihaly Csikszentmihalyi highlight the interaction of creative thinking abilities, motivation, expertise, and contextual circumstances.

10. The "Componential Theory of Creativity" by psychologist Teresa Amabile explores the cognitive mechanisms underlying imaginative thinking. Her study brought to light the importance of intrinsic motivation, domain-specific expertise, and the impact of a person's working environment.

11.Google's policy of giving employees 20% of their workweek for personal projects led to the creation of Gmail and Google News, among other breakthroughs. This method encouraged people to follow interests outside of their jobs, which encouraged creativity.

12.Lego's Creative Play: Lego's dedication to creative play led to the development of items that inspire creativity and originality. Through practical building, the company's "Lego Serious Play" methodology encourages problem-solving and invention.

Unleash the Creativity Within You

It takes exploration and self-discovery to nurture your own creativity. You may access your natural creative talent by encouraging curiosity, accepting different viewpoints, creating an inspiring environment, and learning from mistakes. The road to creative mastery is attainable, supported by research and demonstrated by actual instances from everyday life.

In the end, the fusion of cross-disciplinary learning, accepting restrictions, and mindfulness converges to unlock your creative potential. Your dedication to fostering creativity can shape your career and enable you to contribute to innovation, advancement, and positive change in the world, just as da Vinci's curiosity and Jobs' mindfulness characterized their legacies.

Investigating Creativity: Exposing the Heart of Innovation

Innovation grows from the rich ground of creativity, which is the primary force of development, change, and human expression. It is alchemy that transforms imagination into practical concepts, igniting creative responses to long-standing issues and opening up new vistas. Investigating the nature of creativity reveals its many facets and emphasizes how crucial a role it plays in producing novel ideas that transform businesses, societies, and even our way of life.

Understanding the Creative Process:

At its core, creativity is the process of coming up with fresh, worthwhile, and pertinent ideas. Divergent thinking, which examines many alternatives, and convergent thinking, which condenses those possibilities into useful answers, engage in a complex dance. Whether it be in the realms of art, science, business, or daily life, creativity manifests across disciplines and crosses boundaries to take on a variety of shapes.

The Value of Creativity in the Development of Innovative Ideas

The key to innovation is creativity, and the following examples show how crucial creativity is to coming up with ground-breaking concepts:

1. Problem-solving and Unconventional answers: People that are creative can approach challenges from fresh perspectives and come up with unorthodox answers. Alexander Graham Bell's inventive research into sound transmission via electrical signals led to the development of the telephone.

2. Encourages exploration: Creative thinking embraces the prospect of failure as a stepping stone to achievement, encouraging exploration. Thomas Edison's development of the incandescent light bulb involved a number of inventive experiments that led to a game-changing creation.

3. Fostering Adaptability: Creative people come up with creative solutions to deal with changing situations. The business world saw this when Amazon changed its business model from an online bookstore to a major worldwide e-commerce and technology company.

4. Imaginative thinkers challenge conventions and redefine possibilities as they rethink entire sectors. Apple's ascent to global prominence was fueled by Steve Jobs' innovative vision, which completely reshaped how we engage with technology.

5. Technology's Humanization: Innovation devoid of imagination can produce sterile goods. The iPod's user-friendly interface and attractive form serve as a prime example of Apple's design-driven methodology, which combines innovation and creativity.

6. Consumer Perception and Behavior: Innovative marketing techniques affect consumer perception and behavior. Coca-Cola's well-known "Share a Coke" campaign, which imprinted prominent names on bottles, started a worldwide dialogue about the company.

Famous psychologist Mihaly Csikszentmihalyi researched the idea of "flow," a mental state characterized by sharpened focus and total immersion in activities. He discovered that creative people frequently experience flow, a state that encourages original thought.

In his TED Talk, "Do Schools Kill innovation?," Ken Robinson emphasized how conventional educational systems frequently stifle innovation. He supported encouraging creativity in the classroom to generate creative thinkers.

Apple's renowned advertising campaign, "Think Different," highlighted the link between creativity and invention by honoring innovators like Mahatma Gandhi, Martin Luther King Jr., and Albert Einstein.

Google's Innovation laboratories: Google's innovation laboratories, like Google X, are prime examples of the business's dedication to encouraging creative research. The ability to test out novel, inventive ideas led to the development of projects like self-driving automobiles.

Pixar's Creative Process: As shown in the "Toy Story" films, Pixar engages in vigorous collaboration and the study of a wide range of concepts. Their strategy serves as an example of how imagination fosters innovation in the animation industry.

Set the Creative Genie free.

The ability to be creative is innate in humans and is the driving force behind invention. Its importance is shown in the creation of game-changing concepts that mold industries, affect culture, and redefine possibilities. Csikszentmihalyi and Robinson's research findings support the significant influence of creativity on individual potential and society advancement.

As demonstrated by the case studies of Apple, Google, and Pixar, creativity is the key to success in an innovation-driven economy. It serves as a blank slate for creative concepts, the engine that powers breakthrough innovations, and the thread that ties the fabric of visionary achievements together.

Explore unknown thought-spaces, nurture curiosity, and embrace the creative process. By doing this, you unlock a world of limitless possibilities where innovative ideas are shaped by creative insights, creating a future that is enlightened by human genius.

Liberating your innate creative potential is the goal of Unblocking Creativity.

Human intelligence thrives on creativity, yet even the most inventive people occasionally run against roadblocks that prevent their thoughts from flowing freely. Anyone hoping to tap into their inner creativity and release a wave of original ideas must learn how to get through these creative roadblocks. People can overcome hurdles and access the internal source of inspiration by comprehending the nature of creative blocks and using appropriate solutions.

Untangling the Challenges of Understanding Creative Blocks

Mental impediments that prevent the unrestricted flow of inspiration and ideas are known as creative blockages. They can arise from a number of things, such as self-doubt, burnout, fear of failure, and external demands. These barriers stifle the possibility of ground-breaking ideas emerging by restricting creative expression and innovation.

Unlocking Your Creative Potential: Techniques for Overcoming Creative Blocks

Develop a Growth Mindset: Adopt the growth mindset philosophy, which was put forth by psychologist Carol Dweck. Adopt the viewpoint that difficulties are growth opportunities rather than signs of insufficiency. This change in perspective encourages you to view setbacks as stepping stones on the path to development.

Accept Failure as Feedback: Treat setbacks as insightful advice that directs your creative process. The aphorism of Thomas Edison, "I have not failed. I have just found 10,000 methods that won't work," is a perfect example of the fortitude and knowledge gained by accepting failure.

Practice relaxation and mindfulness: Mindfulness techniques, such as meditation and deep breathing, help to reduce tension and worry, which can lead to barriers in creativity. According to research by psychologist Ellen Langer, mindfulness has a beneficial effect on lowering mental rigidity and fostering creative thinking.

Task Breakdown: Separate creative projects into smaller, more achievable steps. Breaking large projects down into smaller ones encourages a sense of success and progress, whereas undertaking overwhelming projects can cause paralysis.

Change Your Environment: Rearrange your surroundings physically to inspire new insights. By breaking up the monotony of a place you are accustomed with, a change of location can inspire fresh ideas. Steve Jobs was known for holding "walking meetings" to encourage brainstorming.

Engage in creative collaborations to get new thoughts and perspectives. Collaborate, and seek feedback. External criticism can reveal blind spots and spark original ideas. The importance of idea exchange is best demonstrated by Pixar's collaborative approach to filmmaking.

Play and Exploration: Take part in playful pursuits that spark your creativity. Doodling or taking up a hobby helps break through mental barriers, as Albert Einstein once said, "Play is the highest kind of research."

Limit Self-Critique While Brainstorming: Put off self-criticism while brainstorming. Self-censorship and overanalysis might choke off developing thoughts. Create ideas without restriction, then develop and assess them.

In a study on children's and adults' creative thinking, psychologist George Land found that it declines with age. The study emphasized the value of encouraging creativity and implementing techniques to get beyond mental obstacles.

According to Daniel Kahneman's "dual-process theory," there are two different ways of thinking: System 1 (intuitive, rapid) and System 2 (analytical, sluggish). When System 2 overanalyzes, it can stifle the original, unplanned thoughts that System 1 has encouraged.

J.K. Rowling's Rejection: Prior to having her book approved, the Harry Potter series author received a number of rejections. Her fortitude in the face of obstacles serves as a reminder of the value of pushing through obstacles and enduring.

Pixar's Problems with "Toy Story 2": During "Toy Story 2's" production, a technical error almost led to the whole deletion of the movie. The creative team at Pixar shown incredible inventiveness and determination to save their work rather than giving in to panic, demonstrating the strength of perseverance.

The "blank canvas syndrome," a type of creativity block that results from the fear of beginning a new project, frequently affects visual artists.

The difficulty of making the first impression and the larger difficulty of starting creative projects are similar.

Taking Back Your Creativity

The technique of getting beyond creative obstacles is a complex dance of thinking, tactics, and willpower. Your innate creativity can be freed by realizing the nature of these barriers and putting into practice practical solutions, which will unleash a flood of creative thoughts.

Case studies created by J.K. Rowling, Pixar, and artists dealing with "blank canvas syndrome" serve as examples that even the most brilliant people occasionally experience creative obstacles. You can overcome mental obstacles and open the door for creative thought by accepting failure as feedback, changing attitudes, and developing resilience.

Research by George Land and revelations from the dual-process theory emphasize the flexibility of creativity and the importance of tactics in releasing it. Your innate creativity will bloom when you adopt a growth mindset, practice mindfulness, and cultivate a playful attitude. This will enhance your life and add to the tapestry of human inventiveness.

Let's continue to examine the idea of accepting failure as feedback, changing viewpoints, and developing resilience to open the door to creative thinking that is backed by reliable evidence. These trustworthy sources emphasize the interdependence of accepting failure as feedback, changing perspectives, and developing resilience in the context of encouraging innovative thinking.

According to research in the Harvard Business Review, companies that encourage their staff to see failure as a source of feedback are more likely to have an innovative culture. In the long term, more successful inventions can result from recognizing and learning from failure, according to the paper.

In a similar vein, Forbes emphasizes the notion that failure offers useful information for advancement and innovation. It makes reference to MIT Sloan Management Review research that concluded effective innovation is more likely in companies that embrace failure.

Changing viewpoints can foster creativity and new thinking, according to Psychology Today. It offers data demonstrating that those who can look at issues from several perspectives are more likely to come up with creative solutions.

A Harvard Business Review article examines the relationship between innovation and curiosity, which frequently entails examining fresh viewpoints. According to the article's, those who are inquisitive are more likely to come up with novel ideas.

The American Psychological Association also talks about the value of resilience while dealing with adversity. It cites research demonstrating that resilience can be built upon and is associated with improved problem-solving and creative thinking.

Forbes emphasizes the importance of resilience in creative thinking and cites studies that demonstrate how people who bounce back from failures approach issues with new ideas and inventive solutions.

Individuals and organizations can open the door for creative and new solutions by seeing failure as a necessary step on the road to success, investigating many points of view, and learning how to overcome obstacles.

Interactive Workouts to Spark Your Creativity

Beyond only theorizing, actual investigation and participation are necessary to unleash creativity. The goal of these interactive activities is to inspire readers to come up with new ideas, think creatively, and develop their creative thinking. Each task serves as a springboard for invention, enabling you to access your creative thinking reserves and produce original concepts across a range of topics.

1. **Word association exercise:** Write down any words that immediately come to mind when you see a random word. Create a series of connections while exploring the potential paths your thoughts could follow. This activity encourages divergent thought and aids in the discovery of surprising connections.

2. Drawing a primary notion in the middle of a piece of paper and branching out with related concepts will help you create a visual mind map. Connect concepts using symbols, colors, and lines to show the many facets of your ideas.

3. **Reverse Thinking**: Turn a situation completely around. Asking "How can I make this worse?" is a better question to ask than "How can I make this better?" Reversing those bad features will provide creative alternatives.

4. Choose a random thing from your surroundings for the Random thing Challenge. What new use can you give it? This activity challenges you to look at everyday objects in a novel, imaginative way.

5. **Thinking Hats**: Assign multiple "hats" to explore diverse perspectives based on Edward de Bono's method: logical, emotive, optimistic, pessimistic, creative, and process-oriented. You can approach a subject from a different standpoint by wearing each hat.

6. Pose hypothetical "what if" situations in relation to a subject you're working on. What would you do? This activity encourages you to consider potential outcomes, which encourages innovative problem-solving.

7. Look through pictures in periodicals or on the internet for random image inspiration. Choose one that interests you and let your imagination soar. Create a narrative, theme, or notion around the image.

8. Exercise for an Elevator Pitch: Pretend you have 30 seconds to present your idea to a potential partner or investor. Put your idea into a succinct, persuasive pitch that encapsulates it.

9. Exercise on Alternative Uses: Choose an everyday item and come up with as many other uses for it as you can. This task challenges you to consider uses for objects that go beyond their obvious purposes.

10. SCAMPER stands for Substitute, Combine, Adapt, Modify, Put to another Use, Eliminate, and Reverse in the SCAMPER technique. Use these questions to generate creative alternatives to an existing concept or issue.

11. Create an inspirational collage by gathering pictures, sayings, and passages from magazines that speak to you. To make an inspiring collage that ignites your imagination, arrange them on a board or digitally.

12. Exercise in Role Reversal: Pretend you are someone else, such as a fictitious character, a historical person, or even an animal. What strategy would they use to solve the issue you're having? This activity teaches you to look at problems from several angles.

13. Create a metaphor by contrasting your difficulty with something unrelated. This method has the potential to produce original insights and innovative ideas.

14. Use internet tools to create random words with the random word generator. Include these terms in your brainstorming to force yourself to draw unanticipated connections.

15. Select two notions that are unrelated to one another and attempt to integrate them. This practice frequently produces unexpected and creative results.

Building a Platform for Ideas

These interactive tasks work as stepping stones for you as you explore your creative potential. By actively participating in these activities, you cultivate an environment that encourages creative expression and the emergence of new ideas.

Keep in mind that creativity is a muscle that becomes stronger with use. Regular participation in these exercises not only improves your capacity for creativity but also broadens your worldview, allowing you to approach problems from new angles and come up with solutions that are inventive and innovative. So get in, explore, and let your imagination run wild!

Main Points

- Creativity is a Crucial Driver of Innovation and Progress Creativity is a Crucial Driver of Innovation and Progress in Various Domains. Creativity is not just about art.

- The first section of the piece tells the tale of Arjun, a self-published novelist from New Delhi who is on a mission to realize his creative potential.

- Arjun's journey begins with curiosity, which is the entryway to creativity. Curiosity Sparks Creativity. Accept a sense of wonder in the world.

- Arjun developed the skill of focused observation, taking note of small facts and sensations to inspire his imagination.

- Cross-Association Technique: Arjun sparked his imagination and came up with original stories by connecting seemingly unrelated themes.

- Embracing Discomfort: As Arjun did by branching out into several genres, creative progress frequently necessitates stepping outside of your comfort zone and discovering new horizons.

- Arjun's path serves as a reflection of the creative spirit's tenacity. He overcame self-doubt, attained fearlessness, and unleashed his creative potential.

- Innovation legacy: Arjun's tales became a monument to the efficacy of imagination, encouraging people to tap into their own creative potential.

- Techniques for Fostering Creativity: The article offers useful strategies for encouraging creativity, such as encouraging curiosity, accepting different viewpoints, and fostering an environment that is stimulating.

- Reflection and Mindfulness: Meditation and other mindfulness techniques help people become more self-aware and creative.

- Accept Failure: Don't be afraid of failure; it's a step toward success. Learn from mistakes, as Thomas Edison demonstrated in his quest to create the light bulb.

- Constraints can encourage innovation by pressuring you to come up with creative solutions. A good example is Bill Gates' early work on software.

- Encourage the use of brainstorming and diverse thinking to investigate many options.

- Cross-Disciplinary Learning: Learning from many disciplines can give your thoughts new angles.

- These lessons emphasize the value of fostering creativity and the virtues of curiosity, mindfulness, resilience, and the capacity for pain. They also emphasize how learning from many perspectives and disciplines may help to encourage creative thinking.

CHAPTER FIVE

EXAMINING THE ADVANTAGES OF A GROWTH MINDSET

I MAGINE TWO INTREPID TRAVELERS traversing the mind's perilous landscape. Meet Gloria the Grower, a steadfast supporter of the Growth Mindset, and Stan the Stagnant, a promoter of the Fixed Mindset. Let's investigate these attitudes as they move through the life's sceneries.

Stan the Stagnant and His Comfort Zone Castle: Stan the Stagnant lives in a castle constructed entirely of comfort zones. He's the kind of guy who thinks skills and abilities are like the statues in his moat, carved in stone. He boldly declares, attributing his abilities (or lack thereof) to heredity, "I was born this way." He avoids obstacles like a cat avoids water because he believes that if you're not a prodigy, trying is pointless.

Gloria the Grower lives in a forest that is always illuminated by the sun; it is a forest full with promise that is just waiting to be awakened. She enjoys difficulties since they provide a springboard for learning new skills. Her catchphrase is "I may not be there yet, but I'm on my way!" Gloria thinks that growth comes from work and learning, and that obstacles are merely detours rather than obstacles.

The Tale of the Parking Spot: Gloria and Stan went on a parking adventure one day. Only one spot remained in the crowded parking lot when they arrived, necessitating parallel parking. Stan sighed, indicating with his Fixed Mindset that parallel parking was comparable to complex calculus. Gloria, however, saw it as an opportunity to gain new knowledge.

She crammed herself into the space like a puzzle piece with a pinch of humor and a few delicate maneuvers. While the Fixed Mindset closed the doors to his advancement, Stan, on the other hand, circled the parking lot in quest of a location that would be simpler.

The Tricky Toastmasters Meeting: Stan and Gloria encountered yet another obstacle at a Toastmasters event: public speaking. Stan struggled during his speech because of his Fixed Mindset and his conviction that he would never be a compelling speaker. Gloria, though, accepted the difficulty. She practiced, made mistakes, and got better.

Even the most confident presenters first struggled with nerves, the Growth Mindset reassured her, putting her at ease. Gloria developed into a confident speaker over time, which left Stan perplexed.

Understanding Failure: When Stan and Gloria's pasta meals turned into spaghetti disasters, their attitudes became clear. Gloria's Growth Mindset, on the other hand, saw potential in the pandemonium, while Stan's Fixed Mindset handed him a generous amount of self-doubt, muttering that he's "simply not cut out for cooking."

She scoffed at the culinary disaster and vowed to do better. She gradually transformed those mushy noodles into gourmet treats, while Stan's culinary skills remained immobile.

The Big Finish: As our story progresses, it becomes abundantly evident that Stan's Fixed Mindset keeps him imprisoned in a fortress of justifications and unrealized potential. Gloria, on the other hand, is propelled ahead on a voyage of self-discovery and betterment by her growth mindset. In the big scheme of things, life is a constantly changing carnival of obstacles and chances.

Gloria's adoption of the growth mindset gives us the freedom to enjoy the journey, take lessons from the mishaps, and laugh a lot.

So, which explorer are you going to be? Who is in charge—the king of Fixed Comfort or the explorer of the wide Growth domain? Keep in mind that even though Stan and Gloria are fictional characters, the mentalities they stand for are actual and palpable as you travel.

Let's break the bonds of inactivity and set out on a fun, learning-filled journey of our own.

Techniques for Embracing Unlimited Potential

Imagine that you are riding the Life roller coaster, and that the track ahead is full with loops and turns. The Growth Mindset pass is a ticket that will enhance your experience, so hold on. This pass does more than just make the trip more comfortable; it turns every obstacle into a chance for personal development. Let's get into the tactics you can use to get this pass.

1. **Embrace the Power of "Yet"**: Assume you're faced with a challenge you've never encountered, such as putting together a piece of furniture from scratch. But the Growth Mindset adds the essential word: "yet." Instead of closing doors, you open windows to potential future outcomes. The Fixed Mindset would state, "I can't accomplish this." By

admitting that improvement requires time and work, you're paving the way for advancement.

One of basketball's all-time greats, Michael Jordan, notably missed out on playing for his high school team. Instead of giving up, he utilized that loss as fuel to practice harder. He was working tirelessly to acquire the abilities even if he didn't have them "yet."

2. **Accepting challenges as learning opportunities** is similar to accepting puzzles as challenges because easy problems only serve to confirm what you already know. You become a master of riddles by solving difficult ones. Similar to puzzles, challenges in life sharpen your skills and engage your mind.

When selling her novel underwear concept, Sara Blakely, the company's founder, received a lot of no's. She didn't consider those rejections as failures; rather, she saw them as information that motivated her to improve both her offering and her pitch. She accepted every "no" as a challenge and an opportunity to learn.

3. **Accept Work as the Road to Mastery**: Have you ever seen a child learning to walk? Even when they keep falling, do they give up? No! They persevere in attempting till they become skilled. Adults occasionally lose sight of this resiliency. The Growth Mindset recognizes that obstacles are merely stepping stones on the path to mastery and that work is the only way to get there.

As Thomas Edison famously remarked, "I have not failed. I have just found 10,000 ways that won't work." His tireless efforts to develop the light bulb serve as a testament to the efficacy of embracing effort and overcoming setbacks.

4. **Accept Criticism and input:** Even when it's not all positive, the Growth Mindset benefits from input. Criticism is a vital source of knowledge that helps you grow; it is not an attack on your skills. Keep

in mind that progress happens amid difficulties and that diamonds form under strain.

The "Braintrust," a group of coworkers who offer frank input on projects in development, participates in Pixar's creative process. Some of the most adored animated films are a result of this openness to criticism.

5. **Embrace Others' Success as Inspiration**: Imagine someone you know accomplishing a milestone you're aiming towards. The Fixed Mindset may react with enmity or jealousy. However, the growth mindset welcomes that success as proof of what is possible and as inspiration to continue developing.

Oprah Winfrey has publicly praised others' accomplishments. She sees their success as a reminder that there is room for everyone to succeed rather than a danger. Her philosophy is one that acknowledges that success is not a zero-sum game.

6. **Accept Persistence in the Face of Failure**: View failures as plot twists in your life's adventure. Setbacks are not synonymous with failure in the Growth Mindset. They are viewed as passing obstacles that may be surmounted through resiliency and inventive problem-solving.

J.K. Rowling, the author of the Harry Potter books, received countless rejections before finding a publisher. Her perseverance paid off, as her books became viral all over the world. She kept moving forward because of her growth-oriented mindset.

7. Accept the Process Over the Results: The Growth Mindset emphasizes the process rather than the end result. It enjoys the little victories, respects the work put in, and recognizes that progress is a victory in and of itself.

Magnus Carlsen, one of the top chess players in the world, once declared, "I am not a genius; I'm just interested." His outlook places more value on education and growth than on being called talented.

The Growth Mindset is the thread that weaves small moments of growth into the larger tapestry of life. It's the mindset that changes obstacles into chances, failures into successes, and unease into interest.

As you ride your own emotional roller coaster, keep in mind that each tactic you adopt, each lesson you learn, and each obstacle you surmount serves as a brushstroke in the image of your unwavering quest for improvement. So buckle up, keep your Growth Mindset pass close, and be ready to enjoy your boundless potential's thrilling turns and turns.

The value of taking chances and discovering from mistakes

Imagine living in a world without the idea of danger or failure, where you would always be protected from adversity. Although it could seem enticing, this is a place devoid of advancement, development, and the core of the human experience. Risk-taking and learning from mistakes are the threads in life's tapestry that connect creativity, resiliency, and knowledge.

Risk-taking and the ability to learn from failure are two strong forces that can define our journey in the complex mosaic of life. These forces are not merely obstacles in our way; rather, they are stepping stones that open the door to great development and wisdom.

Let's go across the terrain of real-life examples to reveal the profound value of stepping into the arena of risk and embracing the lessons that failures offer as we explore the significance of taking chances and learning from failures.

Utilizing Innovation: The Spark of Progress Comes from Risk

Think of an adventurer who is on the verge of unexplored area. The essence of taking risks—the forerunner of innovation—is choosing to move forward into the uncharted territory. Pioneers are more willing to take risks as they push the envelope, challenge convention, and discover new opportunities, advancing civilization.

The Chief Operating Officer of Facebook, Sheryl Sandberg, entered the usually male-dominated sector of technology. In addition to challenging gender conventions, her decision to leave her comfort zone opened the door for her ground-breaking work in leadership and empowerment.

- Resilience in the Face of Adversity: Lessons from Failure

- Think of a sculptor using a stone block as a canvas. Failure is like the chisel that carves resilience and character. People find the willpower to endure hardship, adapt, and grow stronger in the face of it. Failures teach us what doesn't work, which helps us in our future endeavors.

- Growing in Self-Discovery: Risks as Doors to Personal Development

- Think of the transforming process of a butterfly emerging from its cocoon as a reflection of personal development. Taking chances exposes people to new experiences, stimulating self-discovery, and bringing to light aspects of oneself that would remain concealed inside the boundaries of the familiar.

- The first African-American woman in space, Mae Jemison, chose to follow her ambition in defiance of social norms. She broke through barriers on her voyage into space, but she also inspired young females to embrace their dreams without hesitation.

- Gleaning Gems from the Sands of Failure for Wisdom Cultivation

- Imagine a scholar combing over historic books to find timeless knowledge. Similar to successes, failures have priceless lessons that deepen one's understanding. Analyzing failures, spotting mistakes, and learning from them cultivates wisdom that goes beyond rote memorization.

- One of the most successful investors in the world, Warren Buffett, has experienced his share of failures in the stock market. His strategy for dealing with failures is examining every error to identify its underlying reasons. His unmatched investment savvy is a result of this rigorous thought.

Motivation Unleashed: Risk as an Accelerator for Success

Think of sprinters waiting at the starting line, determination and anticipation written all over their faces. Taking risks gives people that first push they need to achieve their goals. The struggle to overcome challenges inspires inspiration, and the desire for perfection takes on a life of its own.

Tennis legend Serena Williams has continuously improved the rules of the game. Her persistent willingness to taking risks has helped her achieve several Grand Slam triumphs despite setbacks and health issues. Her path serves as evidence of the link between risk and success.

Innovative Problem-Solving: Taking Puzzle Pieces from Failures

To solve a mystery, picture a detective putting together a series of clues. Failures are the pieces of the puzzle that lead to answers. Failure analysis reveals what went wrong, allowing people to adjust their plans, make wise choices, and approach problems from a more enlightened angle.

The creator of Amazon, Jeff Bezos, once referred to failure as "experimentation," and he credits Amazon's success to their culture of accepting failure as an essential component of creativity. This ethos has helped Amazon grow into a major force in global e-commerce.

Risk is the mother of invention: the origin of innovation.

Think about the aviation pioneers, the Wright brothers. To pursue the idea of human flight, Wilbur and Orville Wright put their reputations, time, and resources at risk. They took measured risks, which produced the first successful airplane. The heavens may have remained unconquered if they had flinched away from danger. Their adventure serves as an example of how taking chances spurs creativity by expanding the realm of the possible.

Elon Musk is a contemporary visionary who is renowned for taking bold chances. At Tesla and SpaceX, respectively, he pursued high-risk bets on electric vehicles and space flight. Musk's willingness to take these chances, however, has changed both industries and created new opportunities for people.

Building Resilience: Using Failures as Building Blocks Instead of Obstacles

Imagine a plant in perfect conditions with only soft sunshine exposure. Although it might expand, it lacks the toughness to survive inclement weather. Similar to this, those who protect themselves against failures miss out on the opportunity for progress that comes with difficulty. Failures are excellent teachers because they foster resiliency, adaptability, and the capacity to overcome obstacles.

Risks as a Catalyst for Personal Growth: Broadening Perspectives

Think of your comfort zone as a comfortable bubble where you feel secure and at home. Growth, however, awaits outside of that bubble in new area. By pushing you outside of your comfort zone, taking chances exposes you to fresh perspectives, ideas, and experiences. This broadening of perspectives encourages introspection and personal development.

The youngest recipient of the Nobel Peace Prize, Malala Yousafzai, put her life in danger to promote girls' education in Pakistan. Her brave actions put her in danger but also catapulted her into the public eye on a global scale. Malala's adventurous journey made her a change-advocate and empowered numerous others in addition to herself.

Wisdom Development: Failure as a Rich Source of Knowledge

Imagine a library containing nothing but triumphs. These stories might be motivating, but they don't have the depth that failures do. Failures offer lessons that textbooks cannot: they highlight shortcomings, instill humility, and promote self-analysis. Failure-based learning builds experience-based wisdom.

The failure of Apple co-founder Steve Jobs came from his dismissal from his own business. Instead of giving in to loss, he saw this setback as a chance to advance. Jobs gained important insights into innovation, leadership, and the value of staying true to his vision. Some of Apple's most enduring ideas resulted upon his return to the business.

Risk-taking as a Motivator: Fueling Determination

Imagine a trip free of obstacles—a path where each step is simple. Although it could appear ideal, it lacks the motivation that problems give. By taking chances, you add a healthy dosage of difficulty, which strengthens your resolve and devotion. Overcoming obstacles makes you feel more accomplished and inspires you to pursue excellence.

Media magnate and philanthropist Oprah Winfrey overcame many obstacles on her career. Oprah's experiences, which ranged from a turbulent upbringing to professional setbacks, developed her perseverance and tenacity. Her experience demonstrates how taking calculated risks creates a solid basis for realizing your goals.

Failure as a Breeding Ground for Innovation: Promoting Creativity

Imagine the canvas of an artist—a spotless surface free of paint. Failure paints the picture with unusual colors and patterns, provoking original thought. Failures push you to be creative, investigate different options, and come up with novel solutions that you might not have thought of otherwise.

Thomas Edison experienced numerous setbacks while developing the light bulb. He regarded each failure as a learning opportunity rather than a dead end. Edison experimented with several materials and designs before coming up with a functional and useful light bulb.

Risks and failures are not enemies to be avoided in the big theater of life; rather, they are friends that lead you down the road to development and wisdom. They are the main characters who drive the story of human development, advancement, and fulfillment. The combination of taking risks and being resilient in the face of failure weaves a tapestry rich with accomplishments and wisdom, much like a painter layers colors to produce a masterpiece.

The risks you take and the lessons you gain from failures are what will illuminate your path and define your legacy as you stand at the nexus of the known and the unknown. You not only participate in the symphony of life through these forces, but you also become a composer of its most inspirational tunes.

They increase your capacity for adaptability, creativity, and self-awareness. They serve as a reminder that growth necessitates taking risks and embracing uncertainty. So, keep in mind the imprints left by those who ventured to travel these paths before you as you stand at the fork in the road of risk and failure.

Accept danger as a sign of innovation and failure as a path to knowledge. By doing this, you'll discover the actual meaning of what it means to lead a life filled with depth, meaning, and constant improvement.

The idea of accepting failure as a path to knowledge is profound and has been the subject of significant study and analysis. The following credible sources and statistics back up this assertion:

The Wisdom of Deliberate Mistakes, Harvard Business Review:

This article from the Harvard Business Review explores how accepting setbacks and mistakes can help us learn and develop. It presents evidence to support the idea that people are more likely to become wiser over time if they think back on and learn from their failures.

Similar to this, a study published in Psychological Science investigated the connection between wisdom and regret, which frequently results from failure. According to the study, those who have felt regret and have learned from it are more likely to gain wisdom and make wiser choices in the future.

According to a Psychology Today article, failure may be a great teacher and a method to gain insight. Citing personal tales and psychological science, the article emphasizes the significance of accepting failure and learning from it.

Forbes also examines the connection between failure and wisdom, highlighting the fact that mistakes can be instructive learning experiences that promote knowledge and personal development. It makes reference to studies showing that people who admit their mistakes have larger worldviews.

The American Psychological Association similarly argues how growing from failure can result in insight and personal development. It cites research that suggests people who think about their failures are more likely to become resilient, adaptable, and wiser.

These reliable sources and research support the notion that accepting failure can open the door to knowledge. We obtain insightful knowledge and cultivate the wisdom required to make better decisions and overcome life's obstacles by accepting and learning from our errors and failures.

Practical Training

Here are some hands-on activities for cultivating a mindset for taking chances and growing from setbacks.

1. **Try Something New Weekly**: Set a goal for yourself to try something new every week, whether it's a new meal, a different commute, or a new pastime.

2. Journal for Fear-Exposure and Reflection: Start a journal specifically for tackling your concerns. Every day, list one fear you have about taking chances or failing. Then, confront each worry with a potential benefit or valuable lesson. Write out your worries about taking chances and failing.

Challenge yourself to face each fear on the list one at a time, demonstrating that they are not insurmountable. Keep a record of the chances you've taken, the lessons you've learned, and how these events have helped you become a better person. Make time each day to think back on your experiences.

3. Ask for Feedback Frequently: Encourage honest criticism from close friends, relatives, or coworkers. Recognize constructive criticism as an important tool for development.

4.Set "Stretch" Goals: Aim to push yourself just a little bit past your comfort zone. These objectives promote progress while encouraging you to take sensible risks.

5.Speak Up in Meetings: Even if your ideas aren't perfect, express them at meetings. Accept the risk of participating and take advice from the feedback you get.

6.Talk to those who have taken risks in order to learn from their experiences. Find the lessons you can learn from their adventures by paying attention to their stories, accomplishments, and failures.

7.Try different approaches to problem-solving: When faced with a dilemma, come up with a variety of answers, even if they appear outlandish. Accept the danger of attempting a novel strategy and see what you discover.

8.Visualize Successful Outcomes: Use positive visualization to picture the good results of your risks. This routine fosters confidence in your capacity to overcome obstacles.

9.Practice mindfulness: Accept the moment as it is and let go of your fear of failing. By helping you concentrate on the experience rather than the possible outcome, mindfulness can help you lower anxiety.

10.Analyze your role models to find those who have taken chances and learned from their mistakes. Learn from their experiences, then apply the lessons to your own path.

11.One Step Beyond Comfort: Set a goal for yourself to take one small step beyond of your comfort zone every day. These modest actions strengthen your capacity for taking risks, whether it's talking to a complete stranger or offering to help with a project you've never taken on before.

12.Find a recent success, either personal or professional, and reverse engineer it. Analyze the risks you took along the road and retrace the actions that led to that success. This exercise emphasizes the advantageous results of prudent risk-taking.

13.Set aside a specific period of time for failure-focused brainstorming when considering new projects or ideas. Instead of putting them all into practice, the objective is to change your attitude about failure from avoidance to experimentation.

14.These activities can help you continue to cultivate a growth-oriented mentality by encouraging you to take calculated risks and learn from your mistakes. You'll continue to foster a mindset that thrives on difficulties and uses failures as stepping stones toward growth by implementing these workouts into your daily routine.

Major Takeaways

This Chapter examines the distinction between a growth mindset and a fixed mindset, techniques for embracing limitless potential, and the significance of taking chances and learning from failures.

Here are some major takeaways:
- How a Growth Mindset Differs from a Fixed Mindset:

- Gloria the Grower is an example of the Growth Mindset, which emphasizes the value of hard work, education, and overcoming obstacles in the pursuit of personal growth.

- Stan the Stagnant, a symbol for the Fixed Mindset, clings to the notion that one's skills and abilities are fixed and shies away from challenges in order to preserve one's self-image.

- The Growth Mindset is characterized by embracing difficulties, learning from failures, and recognizing the possibility for improvement.

- The story of Stan and Gloria's parking mishap, the Toastmasters meeting, and culinary pursuits show how these mindsets react differently to difficulties and setbacks.

- How to Accept Your Limitless Potential:

- Embrace the Power of "Yet": Adding "yet" to the end of "I can't do this" creates room for future development and opportunities.

- Accept Difficult Situations as Learning Opportunities: Difficult circumstances and failures are like puzzles that exercise your brain and improve your skills.

- Accept Work as the Road to Mastery: Work is the road to mastery, and obstacles are stepping stones.

- Accept criticism and feedback: Even when it's not all positive, feedback spurs development.

- Use Other People's Success as Inspiration: Celebrate other people's successes and use them as inspiration for your own endeavors.

- Adopt Persistence in the Face of Setbacks: Setbacks are transient obstacles that can be surmounted through resiliency and inventive problem-solving.

- Value Learning, Growth, and Improvement Over Fixed Outcomes or Labels: Embrace the Process Over the Outcome.

- The Value of Taking Chances and Growing from Mistakes:

- Taking risks and learning from setbacks are essential components of wisdom, progress, and personal growth.

- Taking risks encourages innovation by pushing the envelope, challenging conventions, and investigating uncharted territory.

- Failures act as stepping stones that build resiliency, flexibility, and the capacity to overcome obstacles.

- People like Sara Blakely, Winston Churchill, and Sheryl Sandberg provide as living examples of the value of taking risks and learning from setbacks.

- Taking calculated risks and learning from mistakes fosters creativity, horizon-widening, and personal growth.

- These fundamental ideas and useful exercises provide a window into the process of acquiring a growth mindset, accepting difficulties, and learning from mistakes. You can advance on a road of development, ingenuity, and resiliency by developing a mindset similar to Gloria the Grower's by turning failures into stepping stones for success.

CHAPTER SIX

HOW TO EXERCISE YOUR CREATIVE FACULTIES

ACCEPTING ORIGINALITY

The play of light and shadow on the snow-capped peaks captured my attention on a recent trip to the tranquil Himalayas. I took a notebook from my bag and started drawing the amazing scenery I was looking at. I was able to access a source of creativity at that time that I hadn't used in a long time. It served as a reminder that nature's beauty has a special way of releasing our creative potential. It now hangs in my desk as a continual reminder of the value of embracing our surroundings in order to fuel our creativity.

All creative people, including the legendary individuals who have made an everlasting imprint on history, share this process of unlocking creative potential and igniting the creative flame. Let's examine five exemplary cases of how these people used their imagination to attain greatness:

- Leonardo da Vinci, The Polymath Visionary: A true Renaissance man, Leonardo da Vinci was a prime example of the value of interdisciplinary inquiry. His journals, which are chock-full of inventions, observations, and doodles, are evidence of his voracious curiosity. He specialized in everything from engineering to art, using his knowledge to produce ground-breaking inventions like the flying machine. The versatility of Da Vinci's thinking demonstrates the creative potential of varied interests.

- Maya Angelou: The Poetic Soul: Maya Angelou experienced many difficulties during her life, which inspired her poetry and literature. Despite her challenges, she found her voice and used them as a source of inspiration. Her masterwork "I Know Why the Caged Bird Sings," which touched people all around the world, turned personal suffering into universal truths. We can learn from Angelou's example that overcoming obstacles in our personal lives can lead to creative expression and tenacity.

- Steve Jobs, the co-founder of Apple, is known as the "Innovation Pioneer" because he changed technology via design and creativity. The convergence of technology and liberal arts was a point of emphasis for him. Products created by Jobs that successfully combined aesthetics and usefulness changed entire industries. He demonstrated how innovation can be human-centered by thinking creatively beyond the technical and fusing it with the human experience.

- Marie Curie, The Curious Scientist: Marie Curie's pioneering contributions in physics, chemistry, and radiation were all driven by her unyielding curiosity. Her unwavering dedication to discovering the invisible paved the path for ground-breaking developments. Curiosity is the basis for creative development, as Curie's passion to exploration reminds us.

- Pablo Picasso: The Creative Visionary: Picasso's reputation as a revolutionary artist resulted from his readiness to defy accepted aesthetic conventions. For example, his development of Cubism destroyed conventional perceptions of reality. Picasso's openness to try new things and question accepted wisdom emphasizes how crucial it is to push limits and be open to fresh ideas when developing new works of art.

These icons demonstrate to us how creativity cuts across disciplines and backgrounds. It comes from curiosity, difficulty, cross-disciplinary thinking, and the willingness to challenge expectations. It takes embracing different experiences, utilizing one's own stories, and retaining an unrelenting enthusiasm for exploration to fully realize one's creative potential. We may all go out on our own adventures of self-discovery and innovation, just as da Vinci, Angelou, Jobs, Curie, and Picasso discovered their own special routes to creativity.

The unrelenting curiosity, readiness to embrace various experiences, and boldness to confront conventions shared by creative titans like da Vinci, Angelou, Jobs, Curie, and Picasso are what define them as creative individuals. At the point where passion, curiosity, and resiliency meet, creativity flourishes. One can unleash their own creative potential and leave a lasting impression across a variety of endeavors by embracing curiosity, appreciating diverse viewpoints, and boldly pursuing innovation.

Techniques for coming up with original ideas and using unconventional thinking

By using a mind map, you can graphically arrange your thoughts around a single idea. You can investigate other perspectives and correlations by branching out. For example, J.K. Rowling incorporated complex plots and characters into the intricate plot of the Harry Potter series using mind maps.

According to studies conducted by Tony Buzan, the inventor of mind mapping, this technique improves creativity and memory recall. According to a 2012 study from the University of Vienna, mind mapping improves memory and creativity by using both hemispheres of the brain.

Substitute, Combine, Adapt, Modify, Put to another use, Eliminate, and Reverse are the acronyms for the Bob Eberle-created SCAMPER technique. Use these strategies to bring your idea to life, just like Apple did with the iPhone, which combines the features of a phone, iPod, and internet gadget.

A classic use of the SCAMPER approach is Apple's invention of the iPhone. A study that was published in the "Journal of Engineering Education" in 2014 emphasized the efficiency of the SCAMPER technique in cultivating innovative problem-solving abilities. They blended characteristics from numerous devices, significantly changing how people perceive and use technology.

Introduce a random phrase, word, or idea to your method for coming up with ideas. The Swiss Army Knife, for instance, was influenced by the concept of a "pocket tool chest," according to research published in the journal "Creativity Research Journal," which also emphasizes how adding random aspects encourages creative thinking.

Metaphors and analogies: Making comparisons between seemingly unrelated concepts might reveal novel insights. You can connect your book's theme to something unexpected, opening up new possibilities, much as how Steve Jobs described a computer as a "bicycle for the mind," a metaphor that changed how people view technology's role in their lives.

An analysis of research findings in the "Journal of Experimental Psychology: Learning, Memory, and Cognition" in 2017 showed how analogical reasoning improves the capacity for original problem-solving.

Reverse Thinking: Visualize the exact opposite of what you want to happen. This reversal may open up original perspectives. In order to create the breakthrough e-reader known as the Kindle, Amazon took into account the antithesis of real books.

Reversing assumptions helps people overcome cognitive biases and promotes creative thinking, according to a 2013 study published in the "Journal of Cognitive Psychology." Amazon's Kindle was created by flipping the idea of physical books.

Cross-Pollination: Look into areas of study other than writing. The inventive storytelling company Pixar promoted communication among its staff members from various divisions. Cross-disciplinary collaborations between animators, storytellers, and technological experts are the source of Pixar's inventive storytelling, which has produced ground-breaking movies like "Toy Story."

Cross-functional cooperation promotes original idea development in organizations, according to a 2005 study that appeared in "Organization Science."

Brainwriting 6-3-5: Six participants write three thoughts in a group setting over the course of five minutes while handing their page to the next person. Research in "Creativity and Innovation Management" published in 2003 demonstrated the effectiveness of group idea generation techniques like brainwriting in enhancing creativity.

A team at Samsung successfully applied this method to produce a variety of concepts for a new smartphone design, which enhanced innovation.

Provocation: Question presumptions and established norms. Picasso defied conventional methods to develop his distinctive artistic style. Pablo Picasso's artistic approach violated conventional standards and gave rise to Cubism, revolutionizing the art world.

The Harvard Business Review released an article in 1999 addressing how questioning assumptions and norms encourages creative thinking in people and organizations.

Changes in the Environment: Surround oneself with a variety of stimuli. Businesses like Google create unorthodox workspaces to foster employee creativity and innovation, which helps them succeed. A 2014 article in the journal "Psychological Science" revealed a beneficial relationship between environmental diversity and cognitive flexibility and creative thinking.

Periods of "incubation": Sometimes taking a break from a situation causes your mind to process subconsciously. A well-known instance is Archimedes' "Eureka" moment while taking a bath. Unconscious processing and incubation were examined in a study that was published in "Scientific American Mind" in 2012 on problem-solving and creativity.

Forced Connections: Bringing together disparate ideas to create something new.

In order to build a worldwide hospitality network, Airbnb's founders first started by renting air mattresses during a conference. In 2015, a study supporting the value of forced contacts in fostering creative thinking was published in the "Journal of Creative Behavior."

Utilizing constraints: Placing stringent restrictions forces original thought within bounds. The 140-character limit on Twitter forced users to communicate ideas succinctly, changing social media communication. Robert Austin and Lee Devin's book "Artful Making" goes into great detail about how limitations may foster creativity in companies.

Utilizing these methods can significantly speed up your idea generation process. Examples show how different approaches can foster invention, from the interdisciplinary collaborations at Pixar to the constraint-driven creativity at Twitter. Furthermore, scientific research continually highlights the effectiveness of these strategies, highlighting their potential to revitalize your writing experience.

These real-world instances and study findings demonstrate how these strategies are not simply abstract ideas but also useful instruments that people and businesses have successfully used to encourage innovation and creativity. You can harness the power of these techniques to come up with original and interesting ideas by incorporating them into your cognitive process.

b) How curiosity helps to create creativity

The spark that sparks innovation, also referred to as curiosity, plays a significant role in promoting creativity. Individuals and organizations are motivated to go outside traditional boundaries by their insatiable curiosity about the uncharted, their readiness to ask probing questions, and their desire to reveal hidden truths.

When skillfully used, this natural human characteristic has the power to transform entire sectors, alter entire narratives, and lead to ground-breaking discoveries. With the aid of the most recent research studies that shed light on the cognitive mechanisms underpinning curiosity-driven invention, we will explore real-world examples of both people and businesses in this investigation of the role of curiosity in creativity.

Steve Jobs and the Apple Revolution: As a visionary co-founder of Apple Inc., Steve Jobs is a prime example of how curiosity can lead to invention. His obsessive curiosity about the points where technology and the arts converge led to the creation of ground-breaking items like the iPhone and iPad.

Jobs' insatiable curiosity helped Apple grow from a basement startup to a leading global technology company. He shaped an age of invention by pushing the limits of what was thought to be feasible in consumer electronics through his quest of elegance and simplicity.

The "20% Time" Policy at Google is an example of the company's curiosity-driven policies. Google is known for its inventive culture. The business's "20% time" strategy, which permits staff to use one-fifth of their working hours on personal projects, is evidence of the transforming potential of curiosity.

This strategy gave rise to initiatives like Gmail and Google News, showing how freedom that is curiosity-focused inspires people to pursue their interests and develop solutions that reshape sectors.

Elon Musk's Unconventional Efforts: The entrepreneur and visionary has an insatiable curiosity. His businesses, including as SpaceX, Tesla, and Neuralink, are propelled by a tireless pursuit of technological innovation and a desire to challenge preconceived notions out of curiosity. Tesla's electric cars and SpaceX's reusable rockets are examples of how curiosity may lead to game-changing inventions.

IDEO's Human-centered Design: IDEO, a well-known design consultant, uses its human-centered design methodology to capitalize on curiosity. By understanding end users' demands and embracing curiosity, IDEO creates creative solutions that tackle actual problems. This strategy, seen in initiatives like the redesign of the shopping cart, shows how curiosity inspires empathy-driven creativity.

Dr. Todd Kashdan's Insights: Dr. Todd Kashdan has investigated curiosity's complex effects on creativity. He is a top authority in the field. According to his research, curiosity encourages problem-solving, adaptive learning, and intellectual development. People that are curious are more inclined to welcome ambiguity and engage in exploratory behaviors, expanding their knowledge base and increasing their chances of coming up with original ideas.

Neuroscientific Foundations: Neuroscientific studies shed light on how the brain reacts to curiosity. The brain's reward system engages when we come upon something that piques our curiosity, producing dopamine. This enjoyable experience increases information retention and spurs us to look for additional information. This brain mechanism provides a basis for comprehending how curiosity motivates ongoing learning and creative problem-solving.

Curiosity and Creative Problem-Solving: Research by Dr. Kashdan and his associates demonstrates the connection between curiosity and creative problem-solving. People who are curious approach problems with an open mind, take into account various viewpoints, and are more inclined to try out novel solutions. Curiosity fuels this tendency for unusual thinking, which improves their capacity to develop original answers to challenging issues.

The Contribution of Curiosity to Idea production: According to recent research, curiosity contributes significantly to idea production. Curiosity-driven individuals aggressively seek out new knowledge and various viewpoints to collect a wide range of inputs that can be combined to create novel notions.

This is consistent with the methods used by businesses like Google, where employees' "20% time" for personal hobbies enriches the ideas available for innovative projects.

The persistent beacon of curiosity points people and organizations toward uncharted regions of invention and creativity. Together, with the examples of visionaries like Steve Jobs, the methods used by leaders in the field like Google, and the perceptions of ground-breaking scholars like Dr. Todd Kashdan highlight the transforming power of curiosity.

Exploring your creative potential is a fascinating topic that has been the subject of extensive investigation and analysis. Here are some reliable resources and statistics that can help you realize your creative potential:

- The Harvard Business Review examines five essential qualities that innovative leaders have, which also apply to anyone who want to develop their creative potential. These abilities include networking, experimenting with novel ideas, and challenging the current quo.

- Similar to this, Forbes covers the science of creativity and provides helpful advice for encouraging innovation and creativity in a corporate setting. It offers information on how people might use these concepts to unleash their creative potential.

- In a similar vein, the American Psychological Association offers advice and tactics for maximizing one's creative potential in the article "Finding Your Inner Muse: Tips for Tapping Into Your Creative Potential." It highlights the value of curiosity, tenacity, and accepting difficulties in order to create creativity.

These reliable sources and studies provide insightful advice on how to unleash your creativity. In order to unlock creativity and invention, they emphasize the significance of abilities like challenging the status quo, engaging in mindfulness, allowing the mind to wander, and embracing curiosity and perseverance.

Practical Training

Here are 15 simple activities that spark your creativity and spark your curiosity:

1. Setting aside some time each day to write down inquiries about the world around you is known as curiosity journaling. Ask yourself fresh questions to pique your interest and motivate additional investigation.

2. Select a topic at random from Wikipedia and investigate it thor-

oughly. Give yourself permission to explore similar topics by clicking on links. This activity promotes accidental learning.

3. Choose an item, concept, or subject and set a goal for yourself to ask 20 questions about it. Investigate deeper connections and insights by going beyond the obvious questions.

4. Pick an ordinary object or situation to observe mindfully. Spend a few minutes studying it intently, taking note of minute features you might typically miss. This exercise improves your observational abilities and fosters a sense of wonder about the mundane.

5. Pick a creative activity, such as writing or sketching, within the given creative constraints. Set restrictions, like utilizing only a particular palette of colors or including only certain words. These limitations may inspire creative answers.

6. Imagine that you are someone else, such as a fictional character, historical figure, or an inanimate object. Discover the world from their point of view to learn new things.

7. Take a trip through your neighborhood or a local park on a curiosity walk. Keep a keen eye out for your surroundings as you go. Take note to the minute details, sounds, and interactions that are frequently missed.

8. Read widely and explore subjects that are outside your comfort zone. Read a variety of books, articles, and blogs. Experiencing new concepts and viewpoints piques interest and encourages original thought.

9. Create a physical or digital board to collect unanswered questions you come across in daily life. Visit the board sometimes to look for answers or directions for more research.

10. Discuss potential connections between two topics that appear

to be unconnected to one another. This activity promotes creative problem-solving and lateral thinking.

11. Select a historical event or decision for your alternate reality. Investigate how important factors might have changed to influence the path of history. This activity promotes conjecture and analytical thought.

12. Making a mind map with a major theme or question in mind can help you be more creative. Extend your thinking by posing related issues, queries, and potential connections. Mind mapping encourages visual thinking and reveals surprising connections.

13. Find a new idea or product in a different industry as a model. Think about how you could use its concepts in your own area of interest. The practice promotes the exchange of ideas.

14. Ask "What If?": Put up fictitious situations and make hypothetical assumptions. These open-ended questions promote speculation and challenge your creativity.

15. Reverse problem solving is the process of turning a current difficulty around. Ask how you can make it worse rather than how to fix it. This fresh viewpoint frequently reveals unexpected solutions.

Regular participation in these useful activities can help you develop a curious mentality and stimulate your creativity.

Main Points

1.How to tap into your creative potential highlights the significant role that curiosity plays in sparking creativity. It starts off with a personal narrative about how the Himalayas provided artistic inspiration. The next section of the chapter explores the lives of famous people who have used their curiosity to tremendous success.

2.Exploring Leonardo da Vinci's Legacy Across Disciplines

The journals kept by Leonardo da Vinci are evidence of his endless curiosity. His interdisciplinary approach, fusing engineering and the arts, led to ground-breaking inventions like the flying machine. This illustrates how having a wide range of interests may inspire creativity.

3.The Resilience of Maya Angelou in the Face of Adversity

The difficulties Maya Angelou had throughout life gave rise to her lyrical talent. She demonstrated how hardship can inspire creative expression and resiliency by transforming personal suffering into universal truths.

4.Innovation with a focus on people: Steve Jobs' vision

Innovative devices like the iPhone are the result of Steve Jobs' combination of technology and liberal arts. His human-centered methodology demonstrates how innovation flourishes when curiosity drives exploration of the boundaries between several fields.

5.Unwavering Curiosity: The Pioneering Spirit of Marie Curie

Radioactivity was the subject of ground-breaking discoveries thanks to Marie Curie's insatiable curiosity. Her passion for discovering new things emphasizes how important curiosity is for developing one's creativity.

6.Boundaries and Courage: Pablo Picasso's Revolutionary Art

Cubism was developed as a result of Pablo Picasso's resolve to defy accepted aesthetic conventions. His daring technique demonstrates how creativity grows when limitations are stretched.

These instances highlight how important curiosity is in stimulating creativity. The next section of the chapter presents doable exercises to foster creativity and spark curiosity. The exercises range from forced connections and thought mapping to journaling and embracing adversity. There are fifteen exercises altogether. Each practice aims to pique curiosity and broaden the purview of imaginative thinking.

Here is a quick rundown of the 15 practical exercises:

- Create a habit of curiosity-driven inquiry by setting aside some time each day to write down questions about your environment in a curiosity journal.

- Investigate random Wikipedia topics to engage in serendipitous learning while arousing interest in a variety of topics.

- Create 20 probing questions about a thing, a concept, or a subject to encourage greater investigation.

- Sharpen your observational abilities by carefully examining commonplace things and paying attention to subtleties that are frequently missed.

- Creative Constraints: Engage in a creative project with enforced restrictions to inspire creative solutions.

- Reverse the roles by imagining instances from various angles to promote novel thoughts and perspectives.

- Take slow walks while paying close attention to aspects that are sometimes overlooked and exploring your environment with increased curiosity.

- Read widely to expand your horizons and to pique your curiosity and open your eyes to new viewpoints.

- Create a platform to compile and review unanswered issues from daily life in order to encourage further research.

- Connect Seemingly Unrelated thoughts: Combine thoughts to spark new connections and ideas.

- Alternate Realities: Consider the possible outcomes of different decisions and inspire imaginative thought by speculating on how history may have been different.

- Using mind mapping to visualize ideas might help you come up with new connections and insights.

- Analogous Inspiration: Encourage cross-disciplinary creativity by integrating cutting-edge ideas from several domains into your own.

- Ask "What If?" to stimulate speculative thinking and broaden your creative boundaries.

- Reverse problem solving involves approaching problems by thinking of ways to make them worse, leading to outlandish solutions.

Each activity presents a different method for fostering curiosity and encouraging original thought. People can foster their curiosity, explore fresh ways of thinking, and ultimately realize their creative potential by participating in these exercises.

In highlighting the significance of curiosity in the creative process, the chapter comes to a close. It talks about how curiosity is a potent innovation accelerator that cuts across disciplines and opens up unexplored realms of creation. People can unleash their creative potential and leave a lasting impression in a variety of professions by embracing curiosity and using the practical activities.

TAKE A BREAK

WE HAVE REACHED A mid point of the book. You may like to take a break and give a feedback on this book , in the form of a rating or a review on Amazon or Goodreads . This will help immensely in spreading the message in the reading community.

Besides, your suggestions are incredibly important to my creative process as an independent writer. It not only fuels my passion but also allows me to go deeply into the core of my creative attempts and find the very heart of my writing. I respectfully ask that you think about posting a review / rating for " The Positive Thinking Mindset " in order to gain your useful insights and opinions.

It is not necessary for your review to be in-depth or extensive; even a brief collection of ideas that expresses your true feelings will do. Whether your comments are compliments or constructive criticism, they all serve as important building bricks in my search for ongoing development as a writer and storyteller.

You might prefer to scan the QR Code below using your smart phone.

*Scan This QR Cide with your smart phone and leave a
review and rating for this book*

CHAPTER SEVEN

HOW TO MANAGE FAILURE FEARS

"THE UNCOMPLETED PAINTING"

I started painting as a hobby years ago. I had never taken formal painting classes, but I had always been interested in the world of art. I made the decision to sign up for a local art class one day in order to study and develop my talents.

I started to get really into painting as the weeks passed. I experimented with many methods and styles for hours in the studio. Mr. Reynolds, my art instructor, took note of my commitment and pushed me to work on a sizable, challenging picture.

Such a project intrigued and worried me at the same time. I was concerned that if I tried to create a large painting, I might utterly fail.

I was plagued by the worry that I would produce something mediocre and let both myself and others down.

I mustered up the guts to begin the painting one evening. I imagined a stunning environment with vivid colors and detailed architecture. But when I started painting, uncertainty crept in. The colors clashed, the strokes were sloppy, and my vision looked far from reality.

Months passed by while the picture was unfinished. I would struggle with it for a bit before giving up. The empty canvas began to represent my fear of failing. The fear that I would not be able to realize my vision stopped me.

Mr. Reynolds dropped by my studio one day. He observed the incomplete painting and the disappointment on my face. He told me a personal anecdote instead of correcting me or pressing me harder.

He related an occasion when he spent more than a year working on a painting before deciding it wasn't coming out as he had hoped. He had scraped off many coats of paint and begun again. The outcome was a masterwork that had garnered honors and praise.

Failure is not the end; it is a stage in the creative process, according to Mr. Reynolds. Every error every stroke of the brush teaches us something. Don't let your fear of failing prevent you from speaking your mind.

I felt a strong connection to what he said. I came to see that my incomplete painting was actually a reflection of my artistic development rather as a sign of my failure. Instead of seeing it as an impossible objective, I made the choice to see it as a work in progress.

I picked up the painting again and worked on it with renewed vigor. I accepted every error and stroke as a chance to get better. The painting required a lot of time, patience, and modifications before it finally reached a point where I was happy with it.

I learned a vital lesson about overcoming failure fear after finishing that artwork. I discovered that the pursuit of creativity entails risk and flaws. Growing and success ultimately result from accepting those flaws and pushing past the fear.

Today, I recall that unfinished painting and Mr. Reynolds' advice anytime I feel the fear of failure in my writing or any creative endeavor. It serves as a reminder that failure is not the end; rather, it is a step in the direction of artistic expression and self-discovery.

Embracing Resilience as a Success Factor

Fear of failure, those ominous voices that warn against taking chances, can thwart innovation, slow down advancement, and stunt growth. But it's important to understand that failure is not the end but rather a step on the road to success. In this investigation into the complexity of fear of failure, we'll look at how it affects innovation and offer management techniques.

We'll demonstrate the power of resilience and the transformative potential that develops when we accept failure as a catalyst for progress, supported by real-world examples, case studies, research findings, and insights.

Understanding Failure Fear:

Humans naturally experience fear of failure, which comes from our dislike of ambiguity, embarrassment, and disappointment. It is the worry that our labor will be in vain, our concepts will not come to pass, and our ambitions will stay unfulfilled.

Influence of Fear of failure on Innovation: It can stop creative thinking

Fear of failure can prevent people from exploring novel concepts or questioning social conventions, which can stifle creative thought.

Limiting Risk-Taking: Innovation frequently requires taking risks. The fear of failure can discourage people and organizations from exploring novel ideas and disruptive tactics.

Promoting Status Quo: People who are afraid may prefer the status quo, which keeps them from embracing change and exploring unexplored territory.

Reframe Failure as Learning: Reframe failure as a useful learning opportunity rather than seeing it as the end result. Every failure offers learning opportunities that advance development.

Create reasonable expectations: Set attainable objectives and be aware that not all endeavors will be successful right away. Unrealistic expectations may make failure anxiety worse.

Concentrate on the Process: Change your attention from the outcome to the process. Accept the exploration, education, and personal development that each activity brings.

Building a Growth Mindset: Adopt a growth mindset, which is the conviction that skills can be improved through hard work and study. This kind of thinking promotes perseverance in the face of obstacles.

Gratitude for Work: No matter the outcome, you should appreciate and applaud the effort that went into a project. This encourages a favorable mindset toward experimenting.

Growth mindset research by Carol Dweck demonstrates how it affects achievement and resilience. People who have a growth mentality are more inclined to see failure as a temporary setback and a chance for advancement.

The Persistence of Thomas Edison

Thomas Edison's struggle to create the light bulb is an example of perseverance. I have not failed, he famously declared. I recently discovered 10,000 methods that won't work. Ultimately, Edison's capacity to see failures as advancement resulted in a ground-breaking invention.

WD-40's Mistakes

Failures are a common theme in the history of WD-40, a household lubricant with lubricating characteristics. The name itself denotes the number of efforts it took to create a successful product: "Water Displacement, 40th formula."

Building a Resilient Organizational Culture:

A leader's influence on how a company views failure is crucial. Innovation, taking risks, and growth all benefit from a culture that views failure as a teaching opportunity.

Google Accepts Failure

The "Failures" board at Google lists projects that didn't go as planned. Employees are more likely to take measured risks and learn from losses when there is transparency and acceptance of failure.

Developing Resilience from Fear

When faced with resiliency, fear of failure can drive people and organizations toward development and achievement. Fear can become a motivator for creativity by using techniques like redefining failure, adopting a growth mindset, and applauding effort.

Thomas Edison and WD-40 are just a couple of the instances that demonstrate how embracing failure can transform. According to research by Dweck. You become a beacon of resilience by facing the maze of fear head-on with courage and tenacity—a force that not only overcomes challenges but thrives on the teachings they teach.

Unleashing the Winds of Transformation and Resistance to Change

Humans have a strong tendency to stick with what is familiar, which is a powerful force that can stifle innovation and slow down progress. To develop an innovation culture and welcome new opportunities, businesses must overcome this hurdle. In this investigation of resistance to change, we'll examine typical impediments to innovation, analyze their effects, and offer tactics for getting beyond opposition inside organizations.

We will demonstrate the power of adaptability and the transformative potential that arises when change is handled with collaboration and openness, supported by real-world examples, case studies, research findings, and insights.

Understanding Change Resistance:

When people experience changes in the status quo, resistance to change starts to develop. It is motivated by things like fear of the unknown, losing control, and dependence on regular routines. Although normal, this opposition may prevent the acceptance of novel procedures.

Fear of Uncertainty: Change introduces uncertainty, which makes people afraid of potential negative effects or disruptions. People may be hesitant to embrace innovation because of this concern.

Loss of Control: People may resist change if they believe they will lose control of their job functions or work procedures. The craving for stability is the root of this resistance.

Comfort with the Status Quo: It can be difficult to switch to new strategies when one is accustomed to the current procedures and becomes complacent.

Lack of Knowledge: People may reject change out of skepticism if they are unaware of the causes or prospective advantages.

Methods for Dealing with Change Resistance:

Successful Communication: It is possible to allay worries and anxieties by communicating openly and clearly about the benefits of change as well as its reasons for occurring.

Include and collaborate with employees by asking for their feedback, including them in decision-making, and appreciating their views.

Identify and empower change champions inside the organization—people who are passionate about the change and have the ability to persuade others—so that they can influence others.

Demonstrate Success: Present verifiable examples of change implementations that were successful, highlighting good results and allaying concerns.

Kotter and Schlesinger's research emphasizes the value of tackling opposition early on in the change process. Their "Six Change Approaches" concept offers methods to reduce opposition and promote easy transitions.

Steve Jobs's transformation of Apple

Under Steve Jobs, Apple was able to overcome objections to change. After Jobs returned to Apple, the company underwent a cultural transformation that valued risk-taking, creativity, and cooperation. This change ultimately changed the course of the business.

Failure of Kodak to Adopt Digital Innovation

The cautionary tale of Kodak's refusal to shift in the face of digital photography. The company declined because it stuck to its traditional film industry despite developing digital image technology.

Building an Adaptability Culture:

Organizations that promote adaptation are better able to get over change resistance. Employees are more prepared for altering environments when a mindset that values learning, experimentation, and continual improvement is fostered.

The Culture of Adaptation on Netflix

Its culture of adaptability helped Netflix make the successful shift from a DVD rental service to a streaming platform. The company's supremacy in the streaming market was a result of its willingness to challenge its own business model and adopt digital innovation.

Transforming Opportunity from Resistance

When overcome using tactics like good communication, inclusion, and empowerment, resistance to change can be a problem that becomes a chance for development and creativity.

Research by Kotter and Schlesinger, together with examples from the real world like Apple and Netflix, highlight the transformative impact of overcoming opposition. You become a catalyst for change by negotiating the terrain of resistance with empathy and collaboration—a force that not only overcomes obstacles but also opens the way for creativity to bloom in even the most hostile climates.

Practical Training

1. Recognize Your anxieties: List any specific anxieties you have about achieving your objectives or completing your assignments.

2. Personal reflection: Consider your prior failures and the lessons you took away from them.

3. Setting Goals: When setting goals for your initiatives, be sure to bear in mind that failures are just stepping stones to success.

4. Reframe Failure: Reframe a recent failure as a learning opportunity, highlighting the new information you learned.

5. Process Over Outcome: Pick a project and put more emphasis on the process than the outcome.

6. Growth Mindset Practice: Become more adept at adopting a growth mindset by viewing obstacles from a "learning" angle.

7. Recognize and Celebrate Your Efforts – No matter the result, acknowledge and celebrate your efforts.

8. Practice mindfulness meditation to help you deal with your worry and anxiety.

9. Explore Unconventional concepts: Come up with concepts and test them out while overcoming your fear of failing.

10. Task That Involves Risk: In your artistic or professional endeavors, take a measured risk.

11. Visualize Success: Envision a successful outcome while being aware of any potential roadblocks.

12. Learning from Role Models: Look up those who have succeeded after failing, and study them.

13. Positive Affirmations: Create affirmations that support resilience and dispel failure-related dread.

14. Start a Failure log: Keep a log of your failures, your lessons learnt, and your improvement strategies.

15. Discuss Failures: Discuss the growth possibilities of a recent failure with a dependable friend or mentor.

Keep in mind that the activities are intended to assist you in developing a resilient attitude and overcoming failure-related worries with courage and tenacity. You are welcome to modify and customize these exercises to fit your own requirements and situation.

Main Points

1. Failure as a Stepping Stone: Recognize that failure is a step—not an end—on the path to success.

2. Recognize that the human response to failure anxiety is a natural one.

3. Impact on Innovation: Understand how the fear of failing can stifle innovation and development.

4. Overcoming Limits: Develop the ability to confront self-limiting ideas that fuel failure-related anxiety.

5. Developing a growth mindset can help you embrace failures as teaching moments and build resilience.

6. Process Over Outcome: Reorient your attention from results to the teaching and learning process.

7. Setting Achievable Goals: To control expectations and lessen fear, set attainable goals.

8. Honor Effort: Regardless of the result, be proud of the effort you made.

9. Communication Is Important: Be open and honest when discussing change to allay concerns.

10. Encourage Collaboration: In order to overcome opposition, involve others in the transformation process.

11. Study Role Models: To understand the transformative potential of embracing failure, consider examples like Edison and WD-40.

12. Develop Adaptability: Encourage an adaptable culture to overcome reluctance to change.

13. Share success stories of positive transformation, emphasizing its advantages.

14. Identify change agents who may have a positive impact on others and empower them.

15. Mindset Adjustment: Convert resistance to change into chances for improvement.

CHAPTER EIGHT

HOW TO SURVIVE OBSTACLES ON THE ROAD TO INNOVATION

"THE MOBILE BANKING REVOLUTION,"

A young businesswoman named Nisha lived in Mumbai, India's thriving financial center. Nisha had a strong desire to help marginalized areas access financial services, but she encountered several obstacles in her quest for innovation.

Determine a Serious Issue

Nisha noticed that many residents of isolated communities didn't have access to conventional banking services. To get to the closest bank, they had to travel a great distance, which was both difficult and expensive. She took the first step toward innovation by recognizing this urgent need.

Develop a Growth Mindset.

Despite her lack of prior expertise in the financial sector, Nisha was adamant about finding a solution. Instead of letting her lack of experience stop her, she adopted a growth mentality, thinking that she could learn and adjust as she went along.

Perform market research

Nisha did a lot of market research before starting the project. She went to rural locations, spoke with prospective customers, and learned about their financial needs and difficulties. She was able to modify her idea to fit current needs thanks to her investigation.

Dependable strategic alliances

The requirement for regulatory licenses and relationships with banks was one of the difficulties Nisha encountered. She actively sought collaborations with reputable financial institutions, harnessing their knowledge and resources, rather than viewing this as an insurmountable challenge.

Utilize technology

Nisha was aware of the potential for technology to close the financial services gap for marginalized communities. Together with computer professionals, she created a user-friendly mobile banking app that was accessible even in places with spotty internet.

Overcome Doubt and Resistance

Regulatory agencies and conventional banking organizations were skeptical of Nisha's novel notion. She persisted nevertheless, showcasing statistics and success tales from trial projects to show how the app could potentially reach the unbanked populace.

User-Centric Design as a priority

Nisha put a high priority on user-centric design to make sure her innovation was simple to use and understand. She tested the app's usability with users from various backgrounds and made changes in response to their suggestions to make it simple for anyone to use.

Maintain Your Resilience Despite Obstacles

Nisha experienced many setbacks on her journey, from regulatory obstacles to technical difficulties. She persevered, nonetheless, because of her tenacity and unflinching dedication to her goal. She saw every obstacle as a chance to grow and learn.

Celebrate achievements of all sizes.

Nisha rejoiced at each victory as her mobile banking application gained popularity and started improving the lives of people in under-served areas. These celebrations, whether it was the first transaction or the service's extension to new areas, stoked her enthusiasm for innovation.

Continual Development

Nisha recognized that innovation was a continuous process. She and her team expanded their services to offer new financial options while also regularly monitoring user feedback and updating the app. Their dedication to continuous development insured that their innovation would endure.

Through the example of Nisha, we can see how tenacity, a growth mentality, market research, strategic alliances, technology, user-centric design, resilience, celebrating accomplishments, and a dedication to continuous improvement can help us overcome obstacles on the way to innovation. Her mobile banking revolution not only made financial services more accessible but also gave underprivileged people the power to manage their own finances.

Let's now examine in greater detail the procedures needed to overcome obstacles on the road to innovation.

1.Making an Environment That Encourages Innovation

It is crucial to first and foremost establish the ideal atmosphere for innovation to develop and thrive. Similar to nurturing a garden, creating an environment that encourages innovation allows you to reap the benefits of innovative ideas in plenty. Fostering innovation isn't simply a luxury; it's a need for survival and success in the dynamic world of business and beyond.

2.Understanding the Ecosystem that Encourages Innovation:

A symbiotic combination of elements that promote and magnify innovative thinking, experimentation, and the pursuit of new ideas defines an atmosphere that is innovation-friendly. Such an ecosystem extends beyond the commercial world to include communities, governments, and educational institutions.

3.How to Foster an Environment That Is Innovation-Friendly:

Leadership Commitment: Leaders must set an example of innovation commitment and foster a culture that encourages taking risks. A leadership-driven effort at Google called "20% time," which allows staff members to devote a portion of their workweek to personal projects, sparked innovation.

4.Foster an atmosphere of open communication so that thoughts can flow easily between departments and across hierarchies. The incorporation of collaboration capabilities into Slack facilitated communication while encouraging idea sharing and cross-functional cooperation.

5.Teams with a variety of backgrounds, attitudes, and experiences foster innovation by introducing new ideas. The various skills of the Pixar crew, which included artists and technologists, culminated in ground-breaking animated films.

6.Encourage experimentation and view failure as an opportunity to learn. Failures by Amazon with items like the Fire Phone sparked advancements like the popular Amazon Echo. Encouragement of measured risks fosters an experimental culture.

7.Allocate time and resources for projects aimed at fostering creativity. By allocating a portion of staff time to creative tasks, 3M fostered a culture of original thought.

8.Design physical settings for collaboration that promote impromptu conversations and brainstorming sessions. The design of Pixar's corporate headquarters was intentionally chosen to encourage spontaneous conversations between staff members.

9.Encourage innovation by praising and rewarding creative efforts. IBM's "First Class Patent" initiative rewards staff for submitting patent applications, encouraging a mindset of ingenuity.

10.**Embrace Technology:** Use technology to speed up idea sharing and cooperation. Digital platforms and virtual whiteboards make it easier for remote teams to collaborate, fostering global innovation ecosystems.

11.**Learning and Development:** Make an investment in your ongoing education and professional growth. Google's internal courses, referred to as "Googler-to-Googler," let staff members exchange knowledge and promote a climate of group learning.

WIPO, INSEAD, and Cornell University worked together to create the Global Innovation Index, which rates innovation environments all across the world. The study highlights the link between innovation-friendly policies and economic expansion.

Five fundamental behaviors—questioning, watching, networking, experimenting, and associating—were discovered to be the cornerstones of inventive thinking, according to a study published in the Harvard Business Review titled "The Innovator's DNA." An environment that fosters invention can help to build these attitudes.

Google's Innovation Culture: Google's culture encourages creativity and appreciates taking risks. Projects of the corporation, like Google X, serve as examples of a culture that fosters and supports bold ideas.

Apple's Design-Centric Approach: Steve Jobs' focus on design and user experience is the root of Apple's environment that fosters innovation. This attitude permeates all of Apple's products, including MacBooks and iPhones.

Design Thinking at IDEO: Design thinking, an innovation strategy that emphasizes empathic problem-solving and iterative prototyping, is the lifeblood of IDEO, a worldwide design firm. The climate is conducive to innovation and encourages cross-disciplinary cooperation.

Let's now examine in greater detail how an environment that encourages creativity might help pave the way for innovation.

The Planting of Innovation's Seeds

Creating an atmosphere that is conducive to innovation is not a one-size-fits-all undertaking; rather, it is a dynamic process that changes in response to the changing needs of people, organizations, and sectors. You may foster an environment that is conducive to innovative thinking by putting in place tactics that place a high value on open communication, variety, experimentation, and learning.

The benefits of creating an environment that encourages creativity are numerous. Innovative concepts, game-changing technology, and a legacy of progress that not only improves the present but also changes the future can result from the cultivation of creative seeds within a supporting ecosystem.

Gardening for Creativity: Promoting Innovation Through Organizational Culture

The fertile ground of organizational culture is where the seeds of innovation germinate, grow, and produce their fruit. Companies that value and foster innovation can achieve breakthroughs, become leaders in their fields, and change the face of business.

This investigation digs into the complex interaction between organizational culture and innovation, including case studies and research findings that shed light on how to foster cultures that foster ground-breaking concepts.

Understanding Organizational Culture's Effect on Innovation

The shared values, beliefs, behaviors, and customs that characterize an organization's operations make up its organizational culture. When this culture puts an emphasis on innovation, it creates a setting where workers are free to think freely, take calculated risks, and offer ideas that advance the cause.

Techniques for Fostering a Culture of Innovation:

Aligning their vision and activities with a culture of creativity is a crucial part of leading innovation. The co-founders of Google, Larry Page and Sergey Brin, are an excellent example of this alignment since they have created a culture that values inquiry and invention.

Give employees the freedom and autonomy to own their own ideas and projects. The "15% Rule" at 3M promotes liberty and creativity by allowing employees to devote 15% of their time to personal initiatives.

Open Communication: Encourage open discussion and idea-sharing at all organizational levels. The "Deep Dive" seminars offered by IDEO promote cross-functional cooperation by offering a stage for the fusion of various viewpoints.

Tolerance for Failure: Provide a secure environment for trial-and-error activities. The "Day 1" mindset at Amazon encourages taking calculated risks because it understands that mistakes can yield insightful insights and unexpected innovations.

Build teams with a variety of backgrounds, experiences, and viewpoints. Johnson & Johnson's focus on inclusive innovation is evidence that diversity promotes a vibrant interchange of ideas.

Learning and Development: Invest in continual education to develop the abilities of your staff. The "Googler-to-Googler" program at Google promotes internal knowledge-sharing, which supports ongoing development.

Recognizing and Honoring Innovation: Honor and recognize contributions that are creative. The "Gold Awards" at IBM highlight outstanding breakthroughs and emphasize the importance of original thought.

McKinsey & Company research shows a significant link between innovation and a supportive company culture. Businesses that place a high priority on innovation outperform their competitors in terms of expansion and financial success.

A research titled "The Innovator's DNA" that appeared in the Harvard Business Review identified a number of distinct behaviors as being essential to inventive thinking, including inquiring, watching, networking, experimenting, and associating. An inventive mentality can develop in a culture that praises and promotes these actions.

Apple's Innovative DNA: The company's innovative culture is firmly ingrained in its past. Steve Jobs' dedication to user experience and superior design influenced the company's culture and produced ground-breaking devices like the iPhone.

The "Freedom and Responsibility" culture of Netflix gives staff members the freedom to make choices and take calculated risks. Disruptive business methods and the development of original content are both products of this innovative culture.

Focus on Core Values at Zappos: Zappos places a strong emphasis on its core values, which include "Create Fun and A Little Weirdness," which encourages employees to be themselves. This unique atmosphere fosters innovation and original thought.

Planting the Seeds of Cultural Innovation

Organizational culture and innovation are mutually beneficial partners in a symbiotic relationship. An innovation-focused culture has demonstrable advantages for corporate performance and employee engagement, according to research from McKinsey & Company and Harvard corporate Review.

Businesses like Apple, Netflix, and Zappos serve as examples of how a creative culture can revolutionize an organization. These businesses prioritize innovation and incorporate it into every aspect of their operations, which gives them the flexibility to adapt to market changes, progress technology, and set the standard in their respective industries.

The eventual goal of fostering an innovation-friendly culture is the development of an environment that fosters both the generation of unique ideas and their implementation into useful solutions. When a corporation encourages creativity, it cultivates a legacy of invention that extends beyond its products and services, making a lasting impression on several industries and society at large.

Leading as an Innovation Catalyst: Sparking Creativity

An organization's leaders play a crucial role in determining its innovation trajectory. Their behaviors, attitudes, and business practices have the power to either stoke or quench the creative fires. Effective leaders encourage innovation while also fostering a culture that values taking risks and trying new things. This investigation dives into the complex role of leaders in fostering innovation, providing guidance on how they might support these essential elements and showing case studies and research findings that provide light on the way to creating an innovative culture.

Understanding the Innovation Leader's Role:

The building blocks of company culture are leaders. They set the tone for how people view and approach innovation through their actions and decisions. The amount to which innovation flourishes depends on how committed a leader is to encouraging creativity and encouraging risk-taking.

Techniques for Promoting Experimentation and Risk-Taking:

Set an example for your team by being prepared to take calculated risks and consider novel concepts. Elon Musk's daring projects with Tesla and SpaceX serve as examples of how visionary CEOs spur innovation.

Adopt a Growth mentality: Leaders who have a growth mentality, or the belief that one can learn new skills, inspire their people to see obstacles as chances for learning. Satya Nadella, the CEO of Microsoft, changed the company's culture by encouraging innovation and a growth mindset.

Foster an atmosphere where staff members feel comfortable sharing ideas, taking calculated chances, and failing. Google's study on psychological safety highlighted the importance of this factor for encouraging creative teamwork.

Allocate tools for Experimentation: Give staff members the time, money, and tools they need to try out new concepts. Small teams can collaborate on innovative, experimental projects according to Amazon's "Two Pizza Teams" strategy.

Reward Learning and Adaptation: Rather than concentrating only on results, acknowledge and celebrate the learning and adjusting process. The management at Pixar emphasizes the importance of making errors as a necessary component of the creative process.

Encourage Cross-Disciplinary Collaboration: Promote cross-disciplinary cooperation. In part, Steve Jobs' ability to promote cross-functional synergy among designers, engineers, and marketers is responsible for Apple's success.

Leaders who reframe mistakes as stepping stones to success create a culture that encourages experimentation. Celebrate Failure as a Learning Opportunity. The creator of Amazon, Jeff Bezos, underlines the significance of accepting failure as a necessary component of creativity.

The Boston Consulting Group and MIT Sloan Management Review's research emphasize the connection between leadership conduct and innovation results. It is more likely for leaders to drive successful innovation efforts when they encourage experimentation, grant autonomy, and foster an open environment.

A research by leadership authorities Hal Gregersen, Clayton Christensen, and Jeffrey Dyer looked at how "discovery-driven mindset" leaders encouraged creativity. Such managers fostered an innovative culture by encouraging staff members to explore and learn via experience.

Elon Musk's Innovative and Visionary Leadership: Elon Musk's leadership at Tesla and SpaceX is a prime example of innovation and risk-taking. His bold objectives, like as creating a colony on Mars, motivate staff to push limits and discover uncharted territory.

Microsoft Under Satya Nadella's Leadership, the Company Underwent a Cultural Transformation: From a Traditional Software Company to an Innovation-Driven Tech Giant. His emphasis on empathy, teamwork, and experimentation helped to resuscitate the workplace culture.

Amazon's Reputable experimenting Culture: Jeff Bezos' direction fostered Amazon's renowned experimenting culture. The Kindle, Amazon Web Services (AWS), and the Echo series are examples of projects that demonstrate the company's dedication to innovative thinking and taking chances.

Leaders as Champions of Innovation

In order to foster innovation within businesses, leaders have a transformative role. Their capacity to promote risk-taking and experimentation defines the innovation ecosystem, which in turn affects the capacity of the business to adapt, compete, and grow.

Studies published in the MIT Sloan Management Review and observations made by specialists like Dyer, Gregersen, and Christensen highlight the real influence of leadership style on innovation outcomes. Elon Musk, Satya Nadella, and Jeff Bezos demonstrate how their strategies have stimulated innovation, transformed sectors, and encouraged their teams to think creatively and beyond the box.

Leaders become catalysts for unleashing creative potential, igniting disruptive ideas, and enabling firms to carve out a unique and trailblazing path in a world that is changing quickly when they understand that innovation is not just a departmental responsibility but a cultural imperative.

Practical Training

Let's now go into some real-world activities that can entertain us and foster creativity in their respective fields:

1.Brainstorming sessions for innovations: Invite friends or coworkers to frequent sessions. Every time, offer a different task, and allot a certain amount of time to come up with as many original ideas as you can.

2.Keep a diary you can refer to as "The Failure diary" where you can record your failures, what you learnt from them, and how you intend to use these lessons in the future.

3.Cross-Industry Idea Swap: Choose a sector that is unrelated to your own and come up with ideas on how you may incorporate effective strategies from that sector into your own work.

4.Make a reading list of publications that examine innovation, creativity, and unconventional thinking for the innovation book club. Organize conferences or webinars to discuss the main ideas from each book.

5.Spend a day observing someone in a completely different role or industry as part of a "Day in the Life" immersion. This activity may result in new ideas and inventive connections.

6.Forecast future trends for your industry for the next five years. This activity promotes thinking forward and locating possible areas for innovation.

7.The "No Idea Is Too Crazy" Challenge asks participants to come up with their wildest, most unusual solutions to a given issue. This activity encourages thinking beyond the box.

8.Make a mock pitch presentation for an innovative concept you have, as if you were pitching it to stakeholders or investors.

9.Feedback Loop Workshop: Ask for opinions on your ongoing projects from various angles, focusing on how crucial it is to use feedback to make improvements.

10.Introduce the idea of mind mapping as a method for illustrating relationships between thoughts. For the numerous issues you face, make mental maps.

11.Innovation through "reverse engineering": Give your team an existing product or solution, then challenge them to disassemble it and consider alternate solutions.

12.Give yourself a random word, picture, or quotation and challenge yourself to connect it to one of your current tasks or ambitions. Making unanticipated connections during this practice encourages creative thinking.

13.Ecosystem Observation: Encourage others to notice and record instances of innovation in their day-to-day activities, whether it's a minor tweak to a product or a brand-new service.

14.Play the game "Innovation Detective" in which you must come up with an inventive real-world solution to a made-up issue. This gamified approach can keep you interested while educating you about useful innovation.

15."Greenhouse" Project: Assist yourself in beginning a side project that has no connection to your primary work and is solely for the goal of exploring and learning new things. This project can act as a place for experimentation and a creative expression.

The purpose of these activities is to encourage curiosity, teamwork, and an open-minded approach to problem-solving. You can encourage yourself to actively promote innovation in your personal lives and work surroundings by offering fascinating and useful tasks.

Main Points

1.The role of leadership in fostering innovation: Setting up an environment that is conducive to innovation requires strong leaders. They must set the example for their teams by exhibiting a dedication to innovation and embracing risk-taking.

2.Innovation's cultural foundations: Innovation can flourish only in an environment that is hospitable to it. Employees who work in an environment that fosters experimentation and creativity are more likely to offer ground-breaking solutions.

3.Teams with a diversity of opinions are more likely to come up with novel ideas and solutions. To encourage creative thinking, organizations should value people with different backgrounds, perspectives, and experiences.

4.Psychological safety is essential for promoting innovation. A safe space for experimentation. Employees are more inclined to pursue novel ideas when they feel comfortable voicing their opinions, taking chances, and even failing.

5.Investment in Learning and Development: A conducive atmosphere for creativity depends on ongoing education and skill development. Sharing knowledge among staff members encourages an environment of development and innovation.

6.Promoting a Growth Mindset: Leaders that embrace a growth mindset encourage followers to see obstacles as chances for learning and development. This kind of thinking promotes creativity and taking risks.

7.Accepting Failure as a Learning Experience: Failure should be welcomed as a necessary component of the creative process. Leaders who embrace failure as a teaching opportunity foster an experimental culture.

8.Cross-Functional Collaboration: Interdisciplinarity fosters creativity. Leaders should encourage collaboration between departments so that different viewpoints can converge.

9.Allocating Resources for Innovation: It's critical to allocate resources, including time and money, for experimentation. Fostering a culture of creativity involves allowing teams to engage on creative ideas.

10.Research has demonstrated a direct correlation between leadership conduct and innovation outcomes. Leaders are more likely to drive successful innovation efforts if they encourage experimentation and foster open cultures.

11.Effective leaders inspire innovation inside their organizations. Leaders as Innovation Catalysts. They help to shape the innovation culture by encouraging experimentation, taking risks, and open dialogue.

12.Organizational culture that is innovation-focused: Organizational culture is essential to innovation. Innovation and commercial success result when a culture values innovative thought and empowers staff.

13.Learning to Foster Innovation: Fostering a culture of learning encourages the development of new ideas. Understanding the importance of ongoing learning and adaptation creates a setting that encourages original thought.

14.Empowering people to take ownership of their ideas and initiatives develops a culture of independence and creativity that encourages new thinking.

15.Visionary leaders promote innovation by encouraging their teams to push the envelope and discover uncharted territory. Their strategies transform industries and inspire ground-breaking concepts.

These key insights stress the significance of corporate culture, diversity of viewpoints, experimentation, and ongoing learning in establishing an environment that is conducive to innovation. Organizations can overcome obstacles and cultivate an environment that is conducive to ground-breaking ideas by putting these techniques into practice.

Chapter Nine

What Steps to Take to Advance the Innovation Process

THE ENTIRE PROCESS OF transformation cover turning idea into reality, and invention into influence. As we embark on this journey, we will study the intricate processes, strategies, and fundamental concepts that form the basis for successful innovation.

Phase 1 : Idea generation and opportunity recognition

The innovation process begins with ideation, a process when creativity reigns and ideas are generated. Finding opportunities for innovation requires identifying unmet needs, problems, and market gaps. These three activities are the cornerstones of this phase. The study by Chesbrough and Rosenbloom demonstrated the value of outside sources of innovation, such as collaborations and customer feedback, in promoting the creation of successful new products.

The LEGO company's transformation from a struggling toy maker to a creative powerhouse was largely due to its ideation process. LEGO created LEGO Technic and other innovative product lines as a result of realizing the potential to create more flexible building blocks by paying attention to users and play patterns.

Phase 2: Validation and Concept Development

Ideas take shape and then transform into concepts that are refined and verified. Concepts are assessed in relation to client needs, commercial viability, and technical constraints. Prototypes, polls, and focus groups play a significant role in the concept refinement process. The "Lean Startup" methodology, which Eric Ries promotes, places a strong emphasis on iterative testing and concept validation. Research shows that companies using this method are more likely to achieve product-market fit.

An illustration of concept validation is Dropbox's growth from a simple idea to a billion-dollar company. Before creating the product, the founders initially created a video demonstrating how the concept worked. The overwhelmingly positive response validated their theory and made execution practicable.

Phase 3: Innovation in Business Models:

In addition to the creation of new products, innovation can also involve the revision of current business structures. During this stage, it is important to think about how to make money off the invention by considering things like price, distribution, partnerships, and revenue models. The Harvard Business Review article "Reinventing Your Business Model" by Johnson, Christensen, and Kagermann highlights the importance of connecting your business model with your innovation strategy to foster long-term success.

The transition of Netflix from a DVD rental service to a streaming platform with a subscription is a significant divergence from the company's established economic model. Utilizing digital technologies, Netflix overturned the existing entertainment industry distribution strategy.

Phase 4: Execution and Implementation

Here is where the action really picks up. The innovation process necessitates meticulous planning, resource allocation, and project management to guarantee that the idea is transformed into a viable product or service. Throughout this phase, cooperation, team alignment, and relentless execution are necessary.

The research by O'Reilly and Tushman stresses the challenges of managing innovation within established firms. Striking a balance between innovation and pre-existing structures and processes is crucial for successful implementation. Apple's creation of the iPhone, which combined cutting-edge technology, software, and design, is among the best instances of flawless execution. It needed great organization and preparation to put numerous pieces together into a finished result.

Phase 5: Revision and Feedback

Innovation doesn't end with execution; it's a constant process of progress. It is critical to get consumer input, look at performance indicators, and modify the product or service in order to suit changing needs and stay relevant.

The concept of "continuous innovation" emphasizes the significance of ongoing adaptation and development in order to stay competitive in fast-moving markets. The study by Tidd and Bessant underscores how crucial iteration is to maintaining innovation.

Google's iterative approach to product development is seen in the regular modifications to its software and services. By using user feedback to enhance functionality, companies can make sure that their products respond to shifting consumer tastes.

Phase 6 Expanding the appeal of a popular concept or product is a key component in scaling innovation.

Plans for growth, market expansion, and solutions to issues brought on by a rise in demand are required at this stage. Scalability, according to BCG research, is crucial for the innovation process. Organizations that successfully scale innovation across markets have a greater chance of long-term success.

The development of Airbnb from a website for renting out a single room to a significant participant in the hospitality sector demonstrates the effectiveness of scaling. Thanks to its innovative business model and excellent customer experience, the firm saw great growth and market penetration.

The Symphony of Innovation

The process of innovation is an orchestra of creativity, research, validation, application, and iteration. The knowledge of thought leaders like Eric Ries and well-respected research by Johnson, Christensen, and others offer a roadmap for finishing this difficult journey. Examples from companies like LEGO, Dropbox, Netflix, Apple, Google, and Airbnb demonstrate the range of tactics and the revolutionary potential of successful innovation.

As you embark on your innovation journey, keep in mind that innovation isn't a linear process; it's a dynamic, iterative cycle. Every stage, from conception to scaling, adds to a musical symphony of invention and execution in a world where innovation is the driving force behind change, altering industries, improving lives, and speeding development.

The Heart of Creativity: Idea Generation

The core of innovation is idea generation, a dynamic process that gives new ideas and solutions life. In the realm of fostering innovation and catalyzing groundbreaking transformations, the milieu plays a pivotal role. Within the exploration of ideation, we shall delve into methodologies that nurture ingenuity, underscore the significance of diverse perspectives, and derive inspiration from tangible instances and empirical discoveries.

As we navigate this environment, we will study the art and science of developing ideas that have an impact on businesses, technologies, and cultures. A combination of imagination, observation, and well-structured thought go into idea generation. It is both a science and an art. It signals a change from normal thinking and invites us to form fresh connections, confront assumptions, and explore uncharted territory.

Idea Generation techniques

Brainstorming

Professionals and academics have both created strategies for speeding up this process. Brainstorming is a tried-and-true technique for generating ideas that encourages unrestrained, unfiltered idea generation. Participants can express themselves freely and build on one another's ideas in a safe environment.

Mind maps:

Mind maps visually depict the connections between ideas and concepts. They encourage nonlinear thinking and help to draw attention to connections that might otherwise go unnoticed.

SCAMPER

The acronym SCAMPER, which stands for "substitute, combine, adapt, modify, put to another use, remove, and reverse," invites you to do just that when you think about an idea. This approach promotes novel alterations. To gain fresh perspective, imagine yourself in the shoes of someone else, such as a child, an extraterrestrial, or a specialist in your industry. This approach broadens viewpoints and modifies mental patterns.

Putting meaningless words together with a problem will help you think of original solutions. This strategy broadens the variety of options and promotes lateral thinking.

Provocation

The deliberate act of challenging preconceived assumptions is known as provocation. This approach encourages creative problem solving and innovative thinking. Teresa Amabile's studies on creativity place a strong emphasis on the importance of psychological security and intrinsic drive in the generation of ideas. When people feel encouraged and motivated, their creative thinking develops.

Diverse perspectives

Diverse perspectives are crucial for the creation of good ideas, hence they are significant. People with different backgrounds, experiences, and viewpoints join together to form a tapestry of ideas. This diversity promotes innovation by bringing fresh viewpoints and ideas. From many angles, the renowned design firm IDEO is quite fortunate.

Its diverse teams, which include of designers, engineers, psychologists, and other professionals, work together to develop original solutions that handle various requirements.

The story of Pfizer's Viagra illustrates the importance of several points of view in the generation of ideas. While trying to find out the solutions for heart related ailments the researchers found out that Viagra had the potential to address the erectile disorder. This serendipitous discovery can be attributed to the diverse medical backgrounds of the researchers involved. Their ability to forge connections between seemingly unrelated findings ultimately resulted in a revolutionary product.

Fostering an inclusive environment is paramount in the business world. To fully harness the advantages of diverse perspectives, companies must cultivate an atmosphere that embraces and encourages the participation of all voices.

An environment that is inclusive:

In the pursuit of fostering an all-encompassing milieu, enterprises are tasked with the challenge of constructing an environment that exudes inclusivity and extends a warm embrace to the participation of a myriad of voices. This endeavor, in essence, serves as the cornerstone for harnessing the manifold advantages that emanate from a rich tapestry of diverse perspectives.

This requires breaking down silos, fostering open communication, and respecting opposing viewpoints. Johnson & Johnson's "Diversity and Inclusion" initiatives encourage a society that respects diversity. They place a strong emphasis on the relationship between diversity and business performance as well as its role in encouraging innovation through their "Diversity Value Chain" methodology.

In innovation ecosystems, which encourage cross-functional interaction, information sharing, and idea exchange, diverse opinions develop. These ecosystems support an environment where many voices can flourish and add to the collective creative endeavor. The "20% Time" policy at Google, which permits employees to devote a portion of their workweek for personal projects, is an illustration of an innovative ecosystem that values diverse viewpoints.

The development of services like Gmail and Google Maps was the consequence of this strategy. Idea generation is an orchestration of multiple viewpoints, approaches, and surroundings, or a symphony of voices. Amabile's studies and real-world examples, including Pfizer's Viagra and IDEO, highlight the significance of intrinsic motivation, diversity, and inclusion for the generation of original ideas.

As you embark on your own creative journey, keep in mind that idea creation is a collaborative dance in which every viewpoint adds to the innovative choreography. By accepting other points of view, experimenting with approaches, and fostering inclusive environments, you may orchestrate a symphony of ideas that reverberate with the rhythm of growth and shape the landscape of possibilities.

Validation:

The Crucible of Reliability Validation is the crucial process that transforms hazy notions into realistic ones. It comes between ideation and implementation. The factors that guide innovation are data, insights, and practical viability.

Before continuing in our exploration of validation, we'll lead you through the process of polishing concepts using real-world examples, case studies, research findings, and insights. As we make our way across this terrain, we will discover the value of validation in producing innovation that connects with purpose and impact.

The Benefits of Validation:

Validation serves as a litmus test to separate ideas with potential from those that are impractical. It entails carefully considering concepts, assessing their practicality, and ensuring that they satisfy customer and market demands. Validation lessens the risks associated with hastily pursuing concepts that could not result in the desired outcomes.

As part of the validation process, list the underlying assumptions that underlie your proposal. Your idea is based on these assumptions, thus it's critical to confirm them.

To comprehend your target audience's needs, preferences, and pain points better, conduct market research. The study's findings provide insight into whether your plan genuinely satisfies a demand. To get feedback, engage potential customers through questionnaires, interviews, or prototype testing.

Their comments offer insightful details on the benefits and drawbacks of your idea as well as recommendations for improvements. You can see your idea in action by creating a prototype or minimal viable product (MVP). Utilizing prototypes, you may evaluate functionality, user experience, and general viability.

Pilot Testing:

Present a condensed version of your idea to gauge consumer reaction. Pilot tests reveal potential issues and provide a framework for change. According to research by Eric Ries, author of "The Lean Startup," rapid experimentation and iterative testing are vital in the validation process. This method lowers waste and increases the likelihood of generating an item or service that people would like.

The Airbnb Validation Process Airbnb's Validation Process serves as an illustration of the efficiency of data-driven validation. The proprietors initially created a simple website to rent out air mattresses from their living room. They looked at user behavior and found that people were interested in unconventional lodging options. With this turn toward data-driven validation, Airbnb grew significantly as a participant in the global hospitality sector.

Dropbox's MVP Validation

Dropbox's early success is a result of its MVP Validation. The founders created a film to introduce the concept before creating the product. The video's popularity and positive reviews confirmed consumer demand and helped them carry out their plan successfully.

Iterative Refinement:

Testing is just the beginning of a continuous process of improvement known as validation. The input and insights obtained during validation serve as the foundation for iterations that increase the feasibility of the concept. Google's iterative approach to product development is seen in the company's regular product modifications. By using user feedback to enhance functionality, companies can make sure that their products respond to shifting consumer tastes.

Creating a Validation Culture:

Organizations that support this culture create an environment where data-driven decision-making is the norm. By encouraging idea validation prior to execution, teams are more likely to prevent costly failures. GE's application of the Lean Startup methodology to its innovation efforts. This approach, which emphasizes speedy experimentation and learning, fundamentally altered GE's innovation strategy and culture.

The Path of Reliability Validation is the compass that guides innovation toward dependability and impact. Market research, user feedback, iterative refinement, prototyping, and user involvement all aid in the development of ideas into solutions that address real needs. Understandings from Eric Ries' Lean Startup model and real-world examples, such as Airbnb and Dropbox, show how important validation is for guiding successful innovation.

Keep in mind that when you embark on your journey toward validation, it is a dynamic process rather than a static occurrence. You can develop the skills of an innovator by putting your ideas through thorough testing, including others, and using data-driven insights. You can then plan your course with dependability, purpose, and the opportunity to have a big impact by doing this.

The Heartbeat of Innovation:

Execution Techniques The execution stage is when ideas transition from the world of possibility to the realm of reality. It acts as the connecting factor between ideas and actionable plans, between plans and tangible results, and between aspirations and accomplishments.

In this exploration of execution approaches, we will look at strategies for turning concepts into actionable plans, highlighting the need of iteration, learning from mistakes, and drawing inspiration from real-world examples, case studies, and research findings.

As we maneuver through this environment, we'll master the art and science of putting innovation into practice that has a long-lasting effect on businesses and societies.

The art and science of execution represent a finely tuned equilibrium between the orchestration of resources, meticulous planning, and the unwavering dedication to achieving predetermined objectives. It is a harmonious fusion of scientific methodology and creative finesse. It's an innovative symphony that combines planning, cooperation, and adaptability.

Developing executable Plans from Ideas:

The first stage in developing an executable strategy for your idea is to clearly define your goals. These objectives must to be SMART (specific, measurable, achievable, relevant, and time-bound). Clear goals provide direction for action.

Decide how much money, people, and technology you need to support your creation. Resources must be available in sufficient amounts for an execution to be successful.

Create a plan:

In a complete plan, outline the steps, due dates, and milestones for implementing your invention. A roadmap presents a predetermined path for implementation. Create cross-functional teams with a range of perspectives and skills. Collaboration fosters synergy, innovation, and effective problem-solving.

The research of Robert Kaplan and David Norton emphasizes the need of integrating execution and strategy. Their balanced scorecard system emphasizes how important it is to translate strategic goals into actionable plans that guide implementation.

Iterative Approach and Learning from Failure:

Iteration and learning from failure are the cornerstones of successful execution. Iterative strategies involve optimizing and fine-tuning tactics in response to feedback from the field, while learning from errors enables growth and course correction. SpaceX's design of the Falcon 1 rocket is an illustration of the effectiveness of iteration.

Despite repeated setbacks, the company continued to refine its design, leading to the successful launch of Falcon 1 in 2008. The foundation of SpaceX's succeeding tactics was this approach.

Amazon's failures

Over the course of its history, Amazon's failures have influenced its success. For instance, the Fire Phone was a commercial failure, but the lessons learned from it influenced the design of successful products like the Amazon Echo.

The Agile approach and continuous improvement:

The Agile approach is a powerful tool for implementation, especially in companies with a fast rate of change. Agile prioritizes adaptable planning, continuous improvement, and flexible planning. Thanks to this iterative method, teams can adapt to clients' demands and changing circumstances.

The Agile Transformation at Spotify Spotify underwent a full transformation in terms of how it handled execution. The company decided to implement the "Spotify Model," a management approach that emphasizes autonomy, cross-functional teams, and iterative development. This modification accelerated the development of new products and improved client relations.

Organizational learning culture:

Companies are better at applying innovation when they foster learning. Successful execution is encouraged by a culture that respects experimentation, tolerates failure, and always works to improve.

An illustration of a learning organization culture is Google's "20% Time" program, which permits employees to devote a portion of their workweek for personal projects. This tactic encourages creativity by fostering experimentation and failure-based learning.

By turning ideas into actionable plans, embracing iteration, and learning from mistakes, execution brings potential to life. The Balanced Scorecard framework, the Agile methodology, and real-world examples like SpaceX and Amazon all reinforce the importance of execution methods.

As you begin your own execution journey, keep in mind that execution is a communal symphony. By aligning methods with objectives, fostering a learning culture, and using an iterative process, you may become a conductor of innovation—a force that orchestrates success, shapes industries, and leaves a lasting legacy of accomplishment.

Practical Exercises:

Here are 15 practical exercises to help you navigate the innovation process.

1. Idea Generation Workshop: Host brainstorming sessions with a diverse group of individuals to generate a wide range of innovative ideas.

2. Customer Empathy Interviews: Conduct interviews with potential customers to understand their pain points, needs, and preferences, gathering insights for ideation.

3. Mind Mapping: Use mind mapping tools to visually represent and explore relationships between ideas, fostering nonlinear thinking.

4. SCAMPER Technique: Apply SCAMPER (Substitute, Combine, Adapt, Modify, Put to another use, Eliminate, Reverse) to existing concepts to generate creative variations.

5. Role Reversal Exercise: Encourage team members to take on different roles or perspectives, such as a child or an industry expert, to gain fresh insights into a problem.

6. Random Word Association: Associate unrelated words with a problem to trigger unconventional ideas, expanding the realm of possibilities.

7. Provocation Session: Organize sessions where participants deliberately challenge assumptions and norms to encourage disruptive thinking.

8. Prototype Testing: Create simple prototypes or minimum viable products (MVPs) to gather feedback from potential users and validate concepts.

9. Lean Startup Experiment: Develop hypotheses about your innovation and conduct small-scale experiments to validate or refute them.

10. Market Research Surveys: Design surveys to gather data on customer preferences, market trends, and potential demand for your innovation.

11. Cross-Functional Team Collaboration: Assemble cross-functional teams with diverse skills and backgrounds to encourage collaboration and problem-solving.

12. Iterative Development: Implement an iterative approach where you continuously refine and improve your innovation based on user feedback.

13. Failure Analysis: Analyze past failures, either your own or those of other companies, to extract valuable lessons for innovation.

14. Agile Planning: Adopt Agile methodologies to create flexible project plans that can adapt to changing circumstances and customer needs.

15. Learning Culture: Foster a culture of experimentation and continuous improvement within your organization, encouraging employees to learn from failures.

16.

By incorporating these exercises into your creative process as an independent author, you may strengthen your ability to innovate and produce meaningful work.

Primary Lessons

1. Transformational Process: The innovation process transforms ideas into successful innovations and ambitions into reality.

2. The ideation and opportunity recognition stage, concept creation and validation stage, business model innovation stage, implementation and execution stage, feedback and iteration stage, and scaling and commercialization stage are the six stages of innovation.

3. Since the creative process begins with ideation, it's critical to identify unmet needs, discomfort zones, and market gaps.

4. Research has shown that external sources like customer feedback are essential for the successful creation of new goods.

5. The secret to LEGO's success was that they listened to their customers and developed innovative product lines like LEGO Technic.

6. The development of concepts involves refining and assessing them in light of their commercial viability, customer needs, and technical constraints.

7. By emphasizing iterative testing and validation, the lean startup technique increases the likelihood of achieving product-market fit.

8. Dropbox's concept validation: Prior to executing their plan, Dropbox received encouraging comments on a concept video.

9. Innovation in business models includes rethinking concepts like pricing, distribution, collaborations, and revenue structures.

10. According to the Harvard Business Review, for there to be sustainable growth, the business model must be in accordance with an innovation strategy.

11. According to Netflix's business model innovation, the shift from renting DVDs to streaming them upended traditional distribution infrastructures.

12. Implementation and Execution: Apple's launch of the iPhone serves as an example of how execution requires careful planning, resource allocation, and cooperation.

13. Challenges in Managing Innovation: According to O'Reilly and Tushman's research, it is difficult to combine innovation with current practices and institutions.

14. Feedback and Iteration: Google's iterative product development process emphasizes the importance of continuous adaptation and advancement.

15. Scaling and commercialization: Airbnb's rapid growth serves as an illustration of how effective innovation necessitates broadening reach and addressing growth-related difficulties. These essential ideas emphasize crucial ideas and provide instances from the actual world to support you as an inventor. They also provide a well-organized summary of the invention process.

CHAPTER TEN

HOW TO LEVERAGE INNOVATION FOR LONG-TERM SUCCESS

THE "REVOLUTION IN SUSTAINABLE Farming"

My friend Raj, who lives in rural India, had a dream to make his family's traditional farming methods into a successful business. His quest for long-term success through the use of innovation is a tale of commitment, flexibility, and inventive problem-solving.

Phase 1 : Identifying the Need for Innovation

Raj saw that his family's traditional farming practices were becoming more and more unsustainable. Their way of life was in danger due to unpredictable weather patterns, depleted soil, and rising prices. This epiphany served as the impetus for his unique quest.

Phase 2 : Exploring contemporary agricultural technology

Raj investigated modern farming technologies and dove into study to find solutions to the problems. He learned cutting-edge practices including organic pest control, precision farming, and water-wise irrigation. His revolutionary farming methods started with these discoveries.

Phase 3: Learning through experimentation

Raj chose to experiment on a small area of their farm as opposed to putting all these new techniques into practice at once. By being cautious, he was able to learn from his triumphs and mistakes and modify his methods to fit the unique requirements of their farm.

Phase 4: Investment in Sustainable Practices

Raj committed himself to sustainable farming for the long run as a result of his successful efforts. He made investments in environmentally friendly techniques like crop rotation, composting, and solar-powered irrigation systems. These solutions decreased operational expenses while also conserving resources.

Phase 5: Building Partnerships

Raj understood the value of cooperation in the agricultural industry. He established alliances with nearby farmers, exchanging information and materials. These partnerships gave rise to the potential to negotiate collectively and to reach markets for organic food.

Stage 6: Branding and Marketing

Raj understood the need of successful marketing in a time when consumers were more aware of the source and caliber of their food. He made use of social media to build a brand that focused on organic farming and sustainability.

Phase 7: Market Trends Adaptation

Market trends changed throughout time to favor locally grown food and organic food. Raj responded quickly to shifting consumer expectations by extending his product line. To maintain excellent product quality, he also put in place methods for client input.

Phase 8: Instruction and training

Raj gave local farmers instruction in cutting-edge methods to secure the long-term viability of his inventive farming practices. This helped the neighborhood while also enhancing his standing as an innovator in sustainable agriculture.

Phase 9: Hardiness and Ongoing Development

Disease outbreaks, severe weather, and market changes were still problems, but Raj's resiliency and dedication to invention won out. He viewed these difficulties as chances to hone his techniques and further his innovations.

Phase 10: A Sustainable Success Legacy

Raj's farm continues to serve the area as an example of sustainable agriculture today. His family's livelihood has been protected as a result of his original idea to modernize traditional farming, which also encouraged a community to embrace sustainability and creativity.

Raj's experience serves as an example of how innovation may produce long-lasting success when it is embraced with commitment, adaptation, and a long-term vision. His environmentally friendly agricultural methods not only helped his family but also the environment and the community as a whole. It is evidence of how innovation can help to create a better, more sustainable future.

Navigating the Changing Tides of Business Evolution through Continuous Learning and Adaptation

The path to success in today's fast-paced, constantly changing corporate environment is characterized by ongoing learning and adaptation. The capacity of an organization to change in step with shifting trends, technology, and customer needs determines its ability to stay relevant, innovate, and remain competitive.

We will shed light on the crucial role that learning and adaptation play in defining sustainable success and advancing forward progress by drawing conclusions from well-established research work.

Acknowledging the Imperative

The business environment is a dynamic area that is prone to seismic alterations brought on by technical breakthroughs, consumer preferences, and international trends. While organizations that embrace constant learning and adaptation can use change as a fuel for success, those that remain static run the danger of falling behind.

Maintaining Relevance: Those who change succeed in business. Learning and adaptation make ensuring that a company's plans, goods, and services continue to meet consumer demands and market developments.

Innovation and creativity: A culture of continuous learning supports innovation and motivates staff to investigate fresh concepts, try out new methods, and contribute to the expansion of the company.

Agility and Resilience: Agile firms can react quickly to unforeseen difficulties, interruptions, or opportunities, assuring their resilience in tumultuous times.

John Kotter and Rita McGrath's research emphasizes the value of flexibility and ongoing adaptation in a quickly changing environment.

Kotter's work on "accelerating change" is in line with the requirement for businesses to react quickly to shifting market circumstances.

Nokia's Under-Adapted

Because of its inability to adjust to the smartphone era, Nokia's once-dominant position in the mobile phone business has diminished. Despite dominating its field, Nokia's failure to innovate at the right time contributed to its demise.

The Inability of Blockbuster to Change

A striking illustration of the results of not consistently learning and adjusting is Blockbuster's failure to embrace digital streaming and change to changing consumer behavior. On the other side, Netflix embraced digital disruption and profited from the chance.

Taking Advantage of Digital Transformation

The digital age necessitates a strong commitment to lifelong learning. To be competitive, businesses must keep up with developing technology, data analytics, and digital strategy.

Digital Transformation at Disney

The decision by Disney to transition into a digital company is evidence of how crucial it is to advance in the digital era. The corporation was able to capitalize on shifting trends in content consumption thanks to the debut of Disney+, a streaming service.

Building a Culture of Learning:

A learning culture is what motivates ongoing adaptation. Organizations that support continual knowledge and skill development cultivate a workforce that is prepared to face new challenges.

What is a leader's role?

Leaders are essential in encouraging lifelong learning and adaptation. Setting the stage for organizational growth and success is a visionary and learning-centered leadership.

The Change in Leadership at Microsoft

The evolution of Microsoft under Satya Nadella's direction emphasizes the significance of a leader's influence on an organization's capacity for adaptation. The growth attitude and innovation that Nadella emphasized have revived Microsoft's culture and performance.

Accepting Change's Tide

Continuous learning and adaptability are the cornerstones of long-term success in an ever-changing corporate environment, not just survival strategies. Research by Kotter and McGrath as well as case studies involving Disney and Microsoft highlight the revolutionary potential of agility, creativity, and learning.

Embracing change as an opportunity rather than a challenge will help you become a navigator of progress by incorporating the principles of continuous learning into the fabric of an organization's culture. The capacity to learn, develop, and adapt becomes your compass in the volatile corporate world, pointing you in the direction of a future characterized by expansion, toughness, and enduring relevance.

Innovation Metrics: Getting Around the Landscape of Development

In today's changing business environment, innovation is a revolutionary force that affects how businesses develop. Organizations must assess the effects of innovation and monitor development throughout time if they are to effectively harness its power.

Innovation metrics act as a compass, directing businesses toward ground-breaking concepts and practical results. We'll introduce some important indicators that shed light on the efficacy of innovation activities in this discussion of innovation metrics.

Knowledge of Innovation Metrics:

Innovation metrics are measurable indicators that measure how innovation activities affect the effectiveness and expansion of a business. Businesses can learn more about the efficacy of their initiatives, spot opportunities for improvement, and align innovation goals with larger corporate objectives by monitoring a variety of innovation-related metrics.

Important Innovation Metrics

Revenue from New Products: This indicator calculates the proportion of sales coming from new goods or services that were introduced during a certain time frame. It shows that attempts to innovate have been successful in generating new revenue sources.

Time to Market: This metric measures how long it takes to turn an idea into a product or service that is ready for the market. Faster time to market is a sign of effective innovation processes.

Number of New Ideas Produced: Monitoring the quantity of new ideas produced by staff members reveals the organization's innovative culture and its ability to support creativity.

Rate of Idea Conversion: This indicator determines the proportion of ideas that successfully move from generation to development and launch. A higher rate indicates more skillfully chosen and carried out ideas.

Robert G. Cooper's research on innovation measures highlights their significance. In order to assess success, Cooper's work highlights the necessity of measuring both short- and long-term innovation outcomes.

The 3M 15% Rule

The "15% Rule" at 3M permits employees to devote 15% of their working hours to undertaking creative initiatives that are unrelated to their everyday tasks. This strategy encourages a culture of ongoing innovation and idea creation.

20% Time on Google

The well-known "20% Time" strategy at Google encourages staff members to devote a fifth of their working hours to side projects. The result of this strategy was the development of services like Gmail and Google News.

Return on Investment in Innovation (ROII):

Research and development (R&D) costs and other innovation-related expenses are included in the calculation of ROII, which quantifies the financial returns produced from innovation investments.

Investment in R&D by Samsung

Samsung's significant R&D expenditures have produced a wide range of goods, such as smartphones, televisions, and semiconductor technologies.

Customer approval of new products:

This indicator measures how satisfied customers are with recently launched goods or services. Customer feedback offers insightful information about how well innovation activities match market needs.

Customer Loyalty at Apple

Apple consistently prioritizes user experience and user-centric design, which has led to high levels of consumer loyalty and happiness.

Customer-Centered Innovation from Amazon

High levels of customer happiness and loyalty are a result of Amazon's customer-centric approach to innovation. One-click ordering and Prime are two examples of this approach.

Intellectual property and innovation patents:

An organization's dedication to creating distinctive and valuable intellectual property is demonstrated by the number of innovation-related patents that are submitted for and obtained.

IBM's Prominence in Patents

IBM consistently ranks among the top global patent owners, demonstrating its commitment to cutting-edge research and development.

Charting the Course of Development

Innovation metrics weave together a tapestry of information that direct businesses on their path to transformational success. Cooper's research and examples from the real world, including 3M, Google, Samsung, and Apple, highlight the significance of measurement in fostering innovation-driven growth.

Organizations can obtain a thorough understanding of the performance of their innovation efforts by utilizing metrics that evaluate revenue, time to market, idea generation, and customer happiness. Innovation measurements turn into the compass that points businesses in the direction of unexplored growth areas in a world defined by constant change, making sure that the pursuit of innovation stays both a goal and a quantifiable reality.

Practical Training

Here are some helpful activities that people and organizations may use to promote a culture of ongoing learning, adaptability, and accurate innovation measurement:

1.Conduct recurring workshops where teams examine current market trends, technical developments, and consumer preferences. Encourage conversations about how these developments might affect the industry.

2.Conduct a quarterly SWOT analysis (Strengths, Weaknesses, Opportunities, and Threats) to determine which areas require change. Discuss ways to enhance your strengths and lessen your flaws.

3.Organize innovation workshops where staff members can present and brainstorm ideas for enhancing goods, procedures, or customer experiences. Encourage the development of an idea culture.

4.Promote cross-functional learning by planning meetings where teams can exchange ideas and best practices. This promotes the exchange of ideas and information.

5.Provide staff with access to online classes, webinars, or industry conferences so they can keep current on new technologies and market trends.

Organizational and leadership exercises

1.Alignment of Leadership Vision: Hold leadership gatherings to make sure that everyone is on the same page with regards to the organization's vision of ongoing learning and adaptation. Leaders should express their adherence to these values.

2.Innovation Champions: Designate individuals who will lead the organization's efforts to foster a climate of change and learning within their respective teams as innovation champions.

3.Leadership Development: Offer leadership development that places a strong emphasis on the value of adaptability, innovation, and learning.

Cite instances from case studies, such as Microsoft's transition under Satya Nadella.

4.Feedback Loops: Establish routine feedback processes so that staff members can express their opinions on the organization's flexibility and make suggestions for changes.

5.Innovation Awards: Honor and honor staff members and groups for their creative contributions or successful leadership of adaption initiatives.

Exercises for Innovation Metrics:

1.Hold a session on metrics to inform staff about important innovation indicators including revenue from new products, time to market, and customer satisfaction. Describe their significance and effects.

2.Dashboards for innovation: Construct visual dashboards that show metrics for innovation in real time. Make them available to all workers to promote accountability and openness.

3.Launch a competition motivating teams to increase the Rate of Idea Conversion with the "Idea Conversion Challenge." The group that has improved at the fastest pace receives praise.

4.Analysis of client input: Schedule regular meetings where teams examine client input on fresh goods or services. Talk about the best way to use this input to spur innovation.

5.Analyze the Return on Innovation Investment (ROII) for innovations per year. Determine the areas where innovation investments are paying off and the ones that require change.

These hands-on activities support the article's focus on ongoing learning, adaptability, and efficient innovation measurement. In today's changing business environment, they support firms in developing a culture that emphasizes innovation, adaptability, and the pursuit of long-term success.

Main Points

Here are some salient conclusions.

1.Navigating the Changing Tides of Business Evolution through Continuous Learning and Adaptation

2.Business environment that is always changing as a result of shifting consumer tastes, technological advancements, and international trends.

3.Maintaining Relevance: Growing businesses can adapt their offerings to meet changing consumer demands and industry developments.

4.Innovation and creativity: A culture of ongoing education fosters innovation and gives staff members the freedom to test out novel concepts.

5.Agility and Resilience: Organizations that are adaptable are better able to act quickly in the face of difficulties and interruptions.

6.Visionary leadership sets the tone for an organization's flexibility and expansion.

7.Blockbuster and Nokia are two companies that serve as examples of how neglecting to adapt to changing markets can have negative effects.

8.Disney's transition to digital streaming is an example of how firms must embrace continuous learning in the digital era if they want to remain competitive.

9.Learning Culture: To prepare their employees for ever-changing problems, organizations should promote a learning culture.

10.Microsoft's Leadership: Satya Nadella's influence on Microsoft is an example of how leadership is crucial in fostering constant learning and adaptability.

11.Innovation Metrics: Understanding the Landscape of Development 10. Understanding Innovation Metrics: Innovation metrics are measurable measures that evaluate how innovation activities affect the efficiency and development of a business.

12.Key Innovation Metrics: Metrics including new product revenue, time to market, the quantity of new ideas developed, and the rate of concept conversion offer important insights into the efficacy of innovation.

13.The 15% Rule at 3M and the 20% Time at Google are two rules that encourage staff to set aside time for creative initiatives and promote a culture of ongoing innovation.

14.Return on Innovation Investment (ROII) evaluates the financial gains made from innovation investments, which demonstrates how committed a company is to R&D.

15.Customer satisfaction: As Apple and Amazon have shown, customer feedback measures how well innovation efforts have adapted to market demands.

16.Innovation Patents and Intellectual Property: IBM is a prime example of an organization's commitment to creating original intellectual property in terms of the number of patents it has filed.

17.full View: Organizations can get a full picture of their innovation effectiveness by utilizing innovation metrics.

18.The role of measurement is to keep innovation measurable and act as a compass to guide enterprises toward growth.

These key insights stress the significance of ongoing learning, adaptation, and measurement in attaining long-term success and prospering in a corporate environment that is undergoing fast change.

CHAPTER ELEVEN

HOW BUSINESSES ARE USING INNOVATION

INNOVATIVE JOURNEYS: REVEALING THE Innovation Success Stories of Businesses

Businesses that have successfully embraced innovation serve as models for others and are testaments to the transformative potential of innovative approaches. These businesses overcame obstacles, upended whole sectors of the economy, and reshaped the innovation landscape. In this investigation of case studies, we'll examine the histories of such businesses, examine the tactics they used, and expose the results they attained.

We will illustrate the art of innovation and the potential that lies within the pursuit of fresh ideas, supported by established research work, insights, and examples.

1.Apple: Ecosystem Innovation and Pioneering Design

Due to its dedication to superior design and ecosystem integration, Apple's journey is a masterclass in innovation. Steve Jobs promoted the company's "Think Different" culture, emphasizing creativity, simplicity, and user-centered design.

Techniques Used:

User-Cantered Design: Apple stands apart due to its emphasis on the user experience. Understanding customer needs and developing user-friendly interfaces were fundamental to the creation of products like the iPod, iPhone, and iPad.

Environment Integration: The seamless fusion of Apple products, services, and software produced a unified environment that improved customer comfort and fidelity.

Results Attained:

Revolutionized Industries: The iPhone revolutionized computers and communication, while the iPod altered the music industry.

Apple's dedication to design, quality, and user experience helped to cultivate a devoted client base that anxiously anticipated future releases.

Apple's performance is consistent with Clayton Christensen's research on disruptive innovation. According to Christensen's argument, businesses that concentrate on enhancing already-existing items are vulnerable to disruption from those who offer new solutions.

2. Tesla: Inventing the Future of Electric Mobility

Innovative disruption is best illustrated by Tesla's development from a disruptive upstart to a dominant force in the electric vehicle (EV) market. Elon Musk and the company's inventive spirit helped EVs become more widely accepted.

Techniques Used:

Put Performance First: In addition to being environmentally beneficial, Tesla's EVs were also fast automobiles that changed people's opinions about electric cars.

Consumer Direct Model: Tesla's direct sales strategy did away with dealerships, which streamlined the buying process and improved the consumer experience.

Market Transformation: Traditional manufacturers accelerated their own EV development efforts as a result of Tesla's success.

Innovative Technologies: Tesla's improvements in autonomous driving and battery technology have significantly impacted the automobile sector.

Tesla's trajectory fits with Clayton Christensen's idea of "disruptive innovation." By delivering new technology and a new business strategy that ultimately changed the market, Tesla upended the automotive sector.

3. **Amazon:** Customer Focus and the Evolution of E-Commerce

Amazon's transformation from an online book retailer to an e-commerce giant is a testament to its unwavering commitment to customer-centric innovation. The company's founder Jeff Bezos' emphasis on innovation and long-term growth has been a motivating factor.

Techniques Used:

Customer-Centric Culture: From product development to service provision, Amazon operates with a customer-first mentality.

Innovative Technologies: Amazon's creation of tools like Alexa and Amazon Web Services (AWS) demonstrates its capacity to branch out from e-commerce.

Results Attained: E-Commerce Dominance: Amazon became the top online retailer in the world thanks to its creative business techniques.

Alexa redefined voice-activated technologies, while AWS revolutionized cloud computing.

Amazon's strategy is in line with research on "Blue Ocean Strategy" by W. Chan Kim and Renée Mauborgne. By concentrating on consumer demands and developing creative solutions, Amazon established an uncontested market niche.

4. **Netflix**: Changing the Way We Consume Entertainment

The evolution of Netflix from a DVD rental service to a streaming behemoth demonstrates its capacity for innovation, adaptation, and reshaping entertainment consumption.

Techniques Used:

Digital Transformation: Netflix showed its insight in the change toward digital content consumption by switching from physical media to streaming.

Original Content: Netflix's investment in creating original television episodes and films gave it a special selling point that set it apart from rivals.

Results Attained:

Market Disruption: Netflix's streaming service changed the entertainment industry by upending traditional cable and broadcast television.

Global Reach: Netflix's international growth makes it well-known in many nations, demonstrating its capacity to scale innovation.

The success of Netflix is consistent with the idea of "blue ocean" innovation. Netflix was able to avoid direct competition and consolidate its position of dominance by establishing a new market sector through streaming and original programming.

The Success Tapestry

Apple, Tesla, Amazon, and Netflix are case studies that show how innovation may lead to success. The lessons learned from their experiences highlight the value of approaches like user-centered design, disruptive innovation, customer-centricity, and adaptation.

Innovation has the ability to revolutionize industries, according to research by Christensen, Kim, and Mauborgne and real-world instances. These businesses serve as inspiration, serving as a reminder that the pursuit of innovation is not just about ideas but also about turning those ideas into realities that have a significant impact on businesses and societies.

Getting the Most Out of Innovative Journeys: Implementation Insights

For businesses and individuals looking to embrace innovation and promote transformative change, the case studies of Apple, Tesla, Amazon, and Netflix provide a wealth of valuable insights. These lectures offer useful advice and practical insights on a variety of topics, including disruptive techniques and user-centered design.

In this investigation, we'll break down the most important lessons learned from each case study, highlighting their applicability and providing analysis based on previously published research. These insights serve as a road map for putting similar strategies into practice and negotiating the complex environment of innovation.

1. Apple's Lessons in Ecosystem Integration and Excellent Design

Key Learnings:

Usability-Centered Design Understanding user demands and preferences can help you prioritize the user experience. Create goods and services that satisfy users by streamlining interactions and meeting their expectations.

Simplicity Matters: Make an effort to keep your designs simple. While simplicity encourages accessibility and wide adoption, complexity has the potential to alienate users.

Ecosystem Integration: Establish an interconnected ecosystem of goods and services. This improves user comfort, adherence, and cross-product acceptance.

Don Norman's research on "The Design of Everyday Things" highlights the significance of user-centered design. Norman's ideas are in line with Apple's emphasis on designing user-friendly interfaces.

Relevant Learnings:

User Research: Spend money on user research to learn about the needs, problems, and behaviors of users.

Iterative Design: Constantly improve and iterate on the design in response to user feedback.

Ecosystem Synergy: Look for ways to combine goods and services to improve user experiences.

2. Tesla's Lessons for Market Transformation and Disruptive Innovation

Key Learnings:

Perceptions of the challenge: Challenge established norms and perceptions to upend industry. Introduce new technologies that push the envelope and redefine industry norms.

Focus on Performance: To alter people's perceptions of your product or service, emphasize performance and quality. Superior capabilities can influence consumer preferences.

Introduce novel business models that streamline operations, improve consumer experiences, and provide businesses a competitive edge.

Tesla's journey is consistent with Clayton Christensen's notion of "disruptive innovation." Industries can change as a result of innovations that redefine performance and market dynamics.

Relevant Learnings:

Introduce innovations that provide value and subvert conventions incrementally.

Prioritize Quality: Place an emphasis on providing high-caliber goods and services that go above and beyond.

Investigate Alternative Business Models: Look at new business models that fit with your innovation objectives.

3. Amazon's Customer Focus and Diversification Lessons

Key Learnings:

Create a culture that places a high priority on customer demands and feedback. Customer-centric tactics direct decision-making and spur innovation.

Foster a culture of continual innovation by rewarding fresh ideas, embracing failure, and fostering experimentation.

Using cutting-edge technologies and researching related sectors, diversify your offers. This increases potential for growth and lowers dangers.

The "Blue Ocean Strategy" study by W. Chan Kim and Renée Mauborgne is in line with Amazon's strategy. The key to success is to use customer-centric innovation to carve out uncontested market space.

Customer perceptions: Pay attention to consumer input and follow it to inform product development.

Encourage teams to explore with novel concepts and strategies.

Strategically diversify by looking into new directions that complement your primary competencies and market demands.

4. Netflix's Lessons for Original Content and Digital Transformation

Key Learnings:

Adapt to the digital age by embracing digital transformation to meet the changing needs of customers. Recognize and take advantage of changes in how people consume content and technology.

Create Unique Value: Set yourself apart from the competition by creating distinctive value propositions. In the case of Netflix, the production of original content set them apart from rivals.

Scale Innovation: For an international audience, innovations must be scalable. Give high priority to innovations and tactics that promote broad adoption.

The "blue ocean" innovation theory that Kim and Mauborgne proposed is consistent with Netflix's strategy. One method to avoid direct rivalry is by developing a new market niche through distinctive offerings.

Analyze how digital transformation can improve business services and address shifting consumer preferences.

Find strategies to differentiate your goods or services in your niche to stand out in a crowded market.

Reach a Global Audience: Ensure that your inventions are scalable and have the ability to reach a global audience.

Identifying the Routes of Innovation

The case studies of Apple, Tesla, Amazon, and Netflix draw conclusions from lessons that apply to a variety of contexts and industries.

These teachings emphasize the value of adaptability, disruptive innovation, customer centricity, and user-centered design.

These teachings are supported by research conducted by authorities including Don Norman, Clayton Christensen, Kim, and Mauborgne. These observations serve as a road map for people and organizations trying to find their way through the ever-changing innovation landscape and turn ideas into meaningful realities that reshape industries and change the world.

Main Points

Here are some important conclusions:

1. Case Studies in Innovation: It looks at real-world examples of businesses that have successfully adopted innovation.
2. The User-Centered Design Excellence of Apple: Apple's success is credited to its dedication to ecosystem integration and user-centered design.
3. Tesla's Disruptive Innovation: Tesla challenged perceptions and put performance first to disrupt the vehicle industry.
4. Amazon's Customer-Centric Approach: Amazon's constant focus on the needs of its customers and its diversification have been the main factors in its growth.
5. The digital transformation of Netflix: Netflix reacted to the consumption of digital material and set itself apart through original content.
6. Innovation Transforms: The stories of these businesses show how innovation can change entire industries.
7. User-Centered Design Matters: Apple's focus on the user experience emphasizes the value of creating products that are in line with customer requirements.
8. Simplicity Promotes Adoption: Apple's products' simplicity in design makes them more approachable and generally accepted.
9. Ecosystem Integration Fosters Loyalty: The ecosystem integration of Apple products improves customer convenience and promotes brand loyalty.

10. Challenge Industry Norms: Tesla's success was based on redefining performance in electric automobiles and breaking industry norms.

11. Rethink Business strategies: Cutting-edge business strategies, like Tesla's direct-to-consumer strategy, can give companies a competitive edge.

12. The importance of the consumer is paramount. Amazon's customer-focused culture drives decision-making and ongoing innovation.

13. Promote an Innovation Culture: Amazon's strategy fosters fresh thinking, embraces failure, and encourages experimentation.

14. Strategically Diversify: Amazon's expansion into technology, such as AWS, emphasizes the value of looking into related fields.

15. Adapt to Digital Transformation: Netflix's experience highlights the importance of utilizing technology and adapting to changes in the digital landscape.

These lessons learned emphasize the significance of user centricity, disruptive thinking, customer centric cultures, and flexibility in fruitful innovation journeys. For businesses looking to effectively embrace innovation, the ideas of gurus like Don Norman, Clayton Christensen, Kim and Mauborgne give a strong basis.

Chapter Twelve

Conclusion

EMBRACING **I**NNOVATION AND **G**ROWTH'S Journey

We have now come to the end of our innovation voyage. From this point as we take a close look at the key points explained in the chapters especially from the perspective of innovation, creativity, and growth , we find ourselves at the nexus of opportunity and change.

The chapters that came before this one have revealed a mindful of ideas, tactics, and examples from the real world that collectively shed light on the way to innovation-driven success.

Each chapter has served as a stepping stone in this exploration, from the conception of ideas to their realization, from encouraging creativity within ourselves to creating environments that encourage innovation, from the role of leaders in encouraging experimentation to the metrics that measure progress.

Each chapter has served as a stepping stone in this exploration, from the conception of ideas to their realization, from encouraging creativity within ourselves to creating environments that encourage innovation, from the role of leaders in encouraging experimentation to the metrics that measure progress.

Review and Thoughts: A Look at the Odyssey

Let's pause to consider the chapters that have formed the fabric of this book, each one a thread that adds to the story of development and innovation:

Unveiling The Innovative Mindset

We started this adventure by learning about the fundamentals of the innovative mentality—a mindset that values inquiry, welcomes change, and fosters original thought. We introduced the book's idea and emphasized the importance of cultivating a mindset that results in unmatched achievement in the fast-paced corporate environment.

Making an Innovation Blueprint:

We dug into the skill of creating an innovation-driven plan after laying the groundwork in the first chapter. We created a template that readers can relate to and that embodies the essence of innovation, creativity, and economic success from the introduction to the last chapter.

How to Encourage Creativity in Yourself

We delved deeply into introspection as we uncovered the complexities of fostering creativity inside ourselves. We learned the methods for releasing the creative potential that is dormant within each of us through personal experiences, research revelations, and real-world examples.

Understanding and Unleashing Creativity:

We looked more closely at the characteristics of creativity. We revealed the elements that support original thought and the methods for igniting the flames of originality. We illustrated how creativity serves as the fuel that advances innovation through case studies and research.

We addressed the obstacles that prevent innovation and provided solutions to get around them. We paved the way for establishing a culture that welcomes experimentation and adaptation by addressing the fear of failure and resistance to change.

Creating an atmosphere

That nourishes and fosters creativity: As we studied the significance of developing an atmosphere that nourishes and fosters inventive thinking, the canvas of creativity broadened. We established the importance of teamwork, diversity, and psychological safety in encouraging creativity by drawing motivation from real-world experiences and research discoveries.

Leaders as Innovation Catalysts:

As we looked at the transformative potential of visionary leaders, the role of leadership in fostering innovation came center stage. We emphasized the value of leadership that supports taking risks, trying new things, and never stopping learning through inspirational case stories and well-researched findings.

The Transformation from Idea to Execution: As we examined the complex stages of innovation, the journey from ideation to execution came to life. We revealed the methods that help ideas travel the transforming path toward becoming workable solutions, from concept generation through validation.

Idea Generation and Validation: By analyzing the art of idea generation and validation, we probed further into the core of the innovation process. We demonstrated the methods that encourage creativity and guarantee the viability of new solutions using real-world examples and established research.

Strategies for Execution and Accepting Failure: The curtain opened on the execution stage, where ideas are put into action. We examined methods for transforming concepts into workable plans, putting special emphasis on how failure and iteration play a part in effective execution.

Fear of Failure and Resistance to Change: We also looked at the feelings and difficulties that come along with the journey when exploring the landscape of innovation. We examined reluctance to change and fear of failure, providing methods for dealing with these feelings while advancing the cause.

Measuring Innovation and Accepting Continuous Learning: Innovation metrics provided us with concrete indicators of success and acted as our compass. We looked at the metrics that show how well innovation activities are working, from revenue growth to consumer happiness. We also underlined how crucial it is to keep learning and adapt as the business landscape changes.

Reflection Prompt: Your Individual Odyssey of Development

I ask you to consider your own personal voyage as you stand at this point, having traveled the path of innovation and growth:

Your ingenuity story

Which times in your life stand out as being innovative and creative? Think back to times in your career or personal life when your original ideas resulted in positive change.

Supporting Creativity

How do you feel about your ability to be creative? Have you dared to experiment with new things, travel along uncharted roads, or defy social norms? Accepting creativity is a transformational experience in and of itself.

Overcoming obstacles

Consider instances in your life when you had to overcome obstacles or setbacks. How did you overcome these challenges? Did you see failure as a roadblock or as a springboard for improvement?

Taking the Lead:

Think about the leadership position you hold, both professionally and personally, in your organization. How can you motivate and inspire others to embrace change, take chances, and embrace innovation?

How to Assess Your Progress:

What indicators can you use to gauge your own development and innovation? Think about concrete measures that capture your progress, whether they are based on creative outputs, skill growth, or personal accomplishments.

As we come to a close, keep in mind that innovation is a journey filled with invention, growth, and transformation rather than a final destination. Your unique tale of innovation is still developing, just as this book's chapters have created a narrative of development. The concepts of innovation are common, flexible, and long-lasting, regardless of whether you're a business owner, a leader, or an individual looking to advance personally.

As you continue to explore the fascinating landscape of innovation, let this book act as your compass, source of inspiration, and knowledge bank. Your guides on this voyage will be the lessons, ideas, and tactics you've learned here as you head into a future characterized by limitless opportunities, unexplored regions, and the steadfast pursuit of innovation-driven success.

BEFORE YOU GO

PLEASE, SPARE A MINUTE to rate this book using the star ratings from 1-to-5, that usually pops up at the end of this publication. I appreciate your honest feedback, positive or negative. And if you have an extra moment to spare, could you rate the book on Amazon.

Thank you, and best regards.

Manjul

Special Note:

As most e book readers (including the Amazon Kindle) do not have a great internet browser interface, you might prefer to scan the QR Code below using your smart phone.

*Scan the QR Code with your Smart Phone
and leave a review or a rating for the book.*

REFERENCES

"The Innovator's Dilemma" by Clayton Christensen

"Creative Confidence" by Tom Kelley and David Kelley
"Originals: How Non-Conformists Move the World" by Adam Grant
"Lean Startup" by Eric Ries
"Design Thinking: Integrating Innovation, Customer Experience, and Brand Value" by Thomas Lockwood and Edgar Papke
Websites and Blogs:
Harvard Business Review (hbr.org)
TED Talks on Creativity and Innovation (ted.com)
Fast Company (fastcompany.com)
Stanford d.school (dschool.stanford.edu)
Innovation Excellence (innovationexcellence.com)
Podcasts:
"How I Built This" with Guy Raz: Interviews with founders and innovators discussing their entrepreneurial journeys.
"The Innovation Show" with Aidan McCullen: Explores topics related to innovation, leadership, and creativity.
Innovation Labs and Research Centers:

MIT Sloan School of Management - Innovation Lab (mitsloan.mit.edu/innovators-under-35)

Stanford Center for Innovation in Global Health (globalhealth.stanford.edu/innovation.html)

IBM Research - Innovation Lab (ibm.com/research/innovation)

Professional Associations:

The International Society for Professional Innovation Management (ispim.org)

Product Development and Management Association (pdma.org)

Books by the Same Author

BOOKS BY THE SAME AUTHOR

1
INDIA
A CULTURAL VOYAGE
HTTPS://WWW.AMAZON.COM/INDIA-
CULTURAL-CULTURAL-ETERNAL-
RESURGENCE/DP/B08TZ6TBT2

2
How to Think Ten X-
https://www.amazon.com/How-
Think-Ten-Accelerate-
Positivity/dp/B0BD2XPQCZ

3
Mind Your Mind
https://www.amazon.com/MIND-YOUR-
CULTIVATE-INTELLECTUAL-WELL-
BEING/dp/B0BCXYHVKH

4
The Resilient Mindset
https://www.amazon.com/Resilient-
Mindset-STRENGTH-TOUGHNESS-
ADVERSITY-ebook/dp/B0CBQNN34B

BOOKS BY THE SAME AUTHOR

5	The Innovative Mindset https://www.amazon.com/Innovativ e-Mindset-Innovation-Creativity-Innovators-ebook/dp/B0CJ98N8M2	
6	The Eloquent Mindset https://www.amazon.com/dp/ B0CM3D3VW1	
7	The Clear Mindset https://www.amazon.com/dp /B0CSSQ3MC6/	
8	The Positive Thinking Mindset https://www.amazon.com/dp /B0CSSQ3MC6/	

About the Author

MANJUL TEWARI, A BLOGGER, best-selling author, and versatile writer, is the creative force behind the captivating 'Mindset Mastery Series' available on Amazon.

With an engaging and informative style, Manjul's writings transcend conventional boundaries, enriching the lives of readers worldwide. Delve deeper into Manjul's literary world and discover the transformational power of effective communication and mindset mastery.

Visit the **author's profile on Amazon** to explore the full range of captivating works. Uncover the magic of communication and mindset mastery through the lens of Manjul Tewari's literary adventure.

Printed in the USA
CPSIA information can be obtained
at www.ICGtesting.com
LVHW010301100824
787870LV00010B/416